Trauma Responsive Educational Practices

Trauma Responsive Educational Practices

Helping Students Cope and Learn

MICERE KEELS

ascd
Arlington, Virginia USA

2800 Shirlington Rd., Suite 1001 • Arlington, VA 22206 USA
Phone: 800-933-2723 or 703-578-9600 • Fax: 703-575-5400
Website: www.ascd.org • Email: member@ascd.org
Author guidelines: www.ascd.org/write

Penny Reinart, *Deputy Executive Director;* Genny Ostertag, *Managing Director, Book Acquisitions and Editing;* Susan Hills, *Senior Acquisitions Editor;* Mary Beth Nielsen, *Director, Book Editing;* Jamie Greene, *Senior Editor;* Thomas Lytle, *Creative Director;* Donald Ely, *Art Director;* Lisa Hill, *Graphic Designer;* Kelly Marshall, *Production Manager;* Christopher Logan, *Senior Production Specialist;* Circle Graphics, *Typesetter;* Shajuan Martin, *E-Publishing Specialist*

All web links in this book are correct as of the publication date below but may have become inactive or otherwise modified since that time. If you notice a deactivated or changed link, please email books@ascd.org with the words "Link Update" in the subject line. In your message, please specify the web link, the book title, and the page number on which the link appears.

PAPERBACK ISBN: 978-1-4166-3173-6   ASCD product #122015   n3/23
PDF EBOOK ISBN: 978-1-4166-3174-3; see Books in Print for other formats.

Quantity discounts are available: email programteam@ascd.org or call 800-933-2723, ext. 5773, or 703-575-5773. For desk copies, go to www.ascd.org/deskcopy.

Library of Congress Cataloging-in-Publication Data

Names: Keels, Micere, author.
Title: Trauma responsive educational practices : helping students cope and learn / Micere Keels.
Description: Arlington, VA : ASCD, 2023. | Includes bibliographical references and index.
Identifiers: LCCN 2022046073 (print) | LCCN 2022046074 (ebook) |
  ISBN 9781416631736 (paperback) | ISBN 9781416631743 (pdf)
Subjects: LCSH: Children with mental disabilities—Education. | Affective education. |
  Psychic trauma in children. | Post-traumatic stress disorder in children. |
  School environment—Psychological aspects.
Classification: LCC LC4165 .K39 2023 (print) | LCC LC4165 (ebook) |
  DDC 371.92—dc23/eng/20221107
LC record available at https://lccn.loc.gov/2022046073
LC ebook record available at https://lccn.loc.gov/2022046074

30 29 28 27 26 25 24 23   1 2 3 4 5 6 7 8 9 10 11 12

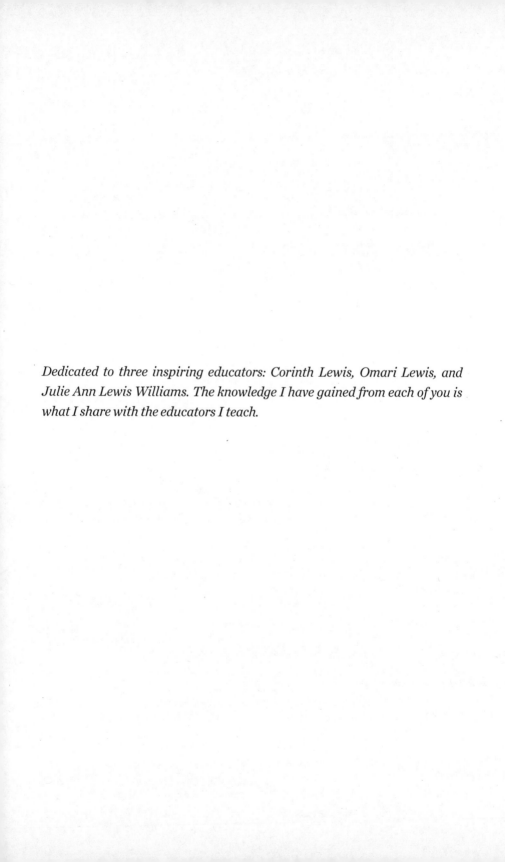

Dedicated to three inspiring educators: Corinth Lewis, Omari Lewis, and Julie Ann Lewis Williams. The knowledge I have gained from each of you is what I share with the educators I teach.

Trauma Responsive Educational Practices

Acknowledgments

I am indebted to all the educators with whom I have worked over the years and their honesty and willingness to share their professional and personal triumphs and struggles.

A tremendous thank you to the TREP Project staff: Thank you Jamilah Bowden, Jessica Nixon, and Stacy Williams for your dedication and passion for developing resources for educators; thank you Alexandra Ehrhardt, Ebony Hinton, Hilary Tackie, and Nick Wilkins for your support in developing resources for our partner schools.

I am grateful for my editors Susan Hills who championed this book and Jamie Greene who patiently supported me through completing the revisions. Thank you to all the ASCD staff members who shepherded this book through to publication.

The research for this book could not have been conducted without generous funding from the William T. Grant Foundation and the Matthew and Luann Jacobs Family Foundation.

1

Introduction to Trauma and Trauma Responsive Educational Practices

No educator can ignore the effects of traumatic stressors on students, and this is especially true for those in schools serving racially and ethnically marginalized or low-income children. Each day, millions of students in the United States carry interpersonal traumas into the classroom from abuse and neglect from the families they depend on for care. Many of these students also carry community traumas associated with the structural violence of concentrated poverty. Some of them also carry the traumatic effects of historical and contemporary race-based oppression. This layering of interpersonal, structural, and historical traumas means that schools serving mostly racially and ethnically marginalized or low-income children must attend to student trauma as an educational justice issue.

We now know that about one out of three students in U.S. classrooms has been exposed to a traumatic event capable of impacting their ability to learn (National Child Traumatic Stress Network, 2008). A wide range of events can cause trauma, including mental, physical, verbal, and sexual abuse; chronic bullying; exposure to chronic community or domestic violence; chronic food and housing insecurity; and many other adverse childhood events. These traumatic experiences conspire to create a host of negative outcomes for children, such as anxiety, depression, aggression, conduct problems, substance abuse, academic failure, and disengagement from school (Cooley-Strickland et al., 2009; Copeland et al.,

2009). When schools provide developmentally supportive responses to these challenges, post-traumatic growth becomes possible.

Because chronic exposure to traumatic stressors and the resulting loss of feelings of safety disrupt students' abilities to regulate their emotions and behaviors, these students often react to even the smallest classroom frustrations with defiant, escalating, or avoidant behaviors. Unfortunately, these dysregulated students are usually met with punitive and exclusionary discipline rather than with trauma responsive interventions. And because school success is one of the primary pathways to escaping oppression, traumatized children who don't succeed in school are often locked in an intergenerational cycle of poverty, violence, and victimization that perpetuates trauma into the next generation (Keels, 2022).

My aim in this book is to encourage the use of trauma as a critical lens through which we can analyze and plan differentiated instruction. Educators who practice differentiated instruction are intentionally reaching out to individuals or subgroups of students by varying their pedagogical practices to meet students' divergent needs (Tomlinson & McTighe, 2006). Differentiation can include differentiated content, learning environment, relationship-building actions, assignments, and work products.

Because children's mental health challenges are especially detectable at schools, these spaces have become mental health assessment and service delivery institutions in addition to places of learning (Leek-Openshaw, 2011). This is critically important as national studies estimate that over 70 percent of children in need of mental health treatment do not receive services (Society for Research in Child Development, 2009). The invisibility of most psychological wounds means that educators are often unaware of how our educational system retraumatizes the most vulnerable and perpetuates intergenerational inequality.

For example, children who grow up with high levels of exposure to chronic neighborhood violence tend to have a harder time processing and controlling their emotions than do their peers who grow up in safe communities. They are also more likely than their peers to struggle with regulating their responses to the emotions and behaviors of others (Groves et al., 1993). This means that a 15-year-old who has grown up amid chronic violence may appear to have the emotional self-regulation of the average 10-year-old. Because that 15-year-old's psychological trauma can be hidden, educators may perceive the behavior as willful defiance and punish the student for not meeting age-appropriate behavioral expectations.

Language and labeling are important aspects of the path to change. By refraining from labeling students and their behaviors as either "good" or "bad," educators can instead focus on the information that behavior communicates. Throughout this book, I use terms like *off-task* and *dysregulated* to label a broad range of challenging student behaviors. It is important for educators to understand that off-task behaviors such as talking out of turn, getting out of one's seat, not paying attention to instruction, behavioral outbursts, and use of profanity may be communicating a student's frustration with academic content or an inability to regulate triggered emotions.

As Figure 1.1 shows, there are three categories of school-based mental health support for students facing trauma. Even though most schools

FIGURE 1.1
Multi-Tiered System of Support

Tier 3: Individualized interventions consist of therapy delivered by clinicians during the school day. Schools tend to have limited capacity for meeting the needs of students identified as requiring these services.

Tier 2: Small-group interventions consist of counseling in small groups focused on developing psychological coping and self-regulation skills. Most schools do not have the capacity to provide enough counseling groups for all students referred for support.

Tier 1: Universal trauma responsive supports consist of policies and practices that promote a safe, socioemotionally informed learning environment in all classroom and nonclassroom spaces throughout the school. Through professional development, educator and administrator coaching, and review of disciplinary and mental health policies and procedures, all schools can implement Tier 1 supports.

lack the mental health resources to meet students' needs for Tier 3 individual therapy or Tier 2 small-group counselling, educators can still significantly reduce cognitive, emotional, and behavorial dysregulation by implementing Tier 1 trauma responsive strategies such as the ones described throughout this book.

Becoming Responsive to Students Coping with Trauma

The path to becoming a trauma responsive educator starts with examining what you know about the underlying causes of dysregulated student behaviors and how your responses contribute to hindering or facilitating post-traumatic growth. Because our perceptions and understanding of the behaviors we see determine how we address them, one of my goals in this book is to help explain the neurobiology of trauma and the resulting cognitive, emotional, and behavioral dysregulation.

If you believe that behavioral dysregulation is a choice, you will more likely perceive students' off-task and acting-out behaviors as willful defiance and respond with punitive discipline. However, the more you understand how challenging behaviors can originate from toxic stress and trauma, the more likely you will be to respond with coregulation—a concept that I will return to often in this book. *Coregulation* is an interpersonal process whereby a caregiver provides ongoing regulatory support during times of stress (Rosanbalm & Murray, 2017). When dysregulated behaviors are met with calming, regulating responses from a trusted adult, children learn how to self-regulate their thinking, emotions, and behaviors.

There are three primary components of coregulation. Though each is beneficial on its own, providing all three results in the best outcomes:

1. Build a warm, responsive relationship through care and affection.
2. Structure the environment to reduce self-regulation demands and provide a buffer against unnecessary stressors.
3. Coach self-regulation skills through modeling, instruction, opportunities for practice, and reinforcement of incremental progress.

When you are challenged by a student's behavior, remind yourself that the behavior is not arbitrary but based on previous experiences and that it serves a function in the present context, even if it is maladaptive (Wolpow et al., 2009). As such, off-task behaviors signal the need for additional instructional, behavioral, and mental health support.

A Brief Introduction to Stress and Trauma

Exposure to stress alone does not lead directly to traumatization, which is caused by stressors that overwhelm our coping resources. There are three general types of stress:

1. **Positive stress** is associated with physiologically and psychologically demanding events that are experienced as motivating or exciting. This kind of stress is within our coping abilities and pushes us to improve our performance or learn something new.
2. **Tolerable stress** is associated with physiologically and psychologically costly experiences that are brief enough or that happen in the context of coping supports so healing can occur before the next potentially traumatic event.
3. **Traumatic stress** is associated with episodic or chronic events that activate or prolong our "fight, flight, or freeze" response system such that they cause physiological and psychological harm.

Not every stressful event is traumatic, though, and not everyone who experiences a potentially traumatic event will be traumatized by it. Almost everyone experiences at least one intensely stressful life event, and most such events, instead of being traumatic, spur the development of new competencies. Stress becomes toxic and traumatic when it is accompanied by a loss of physical, psychological, and emotional safety that overwhelms our ability to cope and we don't have the resources or interpersonal supports to process it.

A **potentially traumatic event** can be a single major event, several moderate events, or an accumulation of repeated small events. **Trauma** is the individual's response to the traumatic event; not the event itself. **Traumatization** occurs when the person does not have enough individual or interpersonal coping resources to restore their sense of safety. Traumatic experiences occurring early in life create **developmental trauma**, which disrupts the development of core cognitive, emotional, and behavioral self-regulation capacities.

When traumatic stress overwhelms our ability to cope, our neurobiology is immediately triggered to respond in a self-protective manner. Depending on our access to coping resources, this neurobiological change can last for days, weeks, months, or years. The longer the changes last, the more damaging they are to development (Perry et al., 1995; Shonkoff et al., 2012). These changes are often not easily observable, and children may appear to be OK in the moment only for the negative effects to deepen over time. The subjectivity of trauma and complexity of traumatization mean that school-based support and intervention rely on educators' abilities to recognize, assess, and respond to student needs.

It is therefore critical to understand that trauma is subjective, traumatization is complex, and treatment is not prescriptive:

- **Trauma is subjective** because of differentiating factors such as age, developmental level, personal sensitivity to stress, and intensity of the stressor (Carlson & Dalenberg, 2000). This means that no two children will experience any potentially traumatic event in the same way.
- **Traumatization is complex** because an individual's maturity, internal coping resources, sources of interpersonal support, and intensity of exposure to traumatic stressors all determine whether traumatization will occur.
- **Treatment is not prescriptive** precisely because trauma is subjective and traumatization is complex; the recovery pathway is specific to each individual. Recovery is based on contextual and cultural understandings of the community that the school serves and some level of individualized understanding of each student's stressors and coping resources.

Chronic Trauma

Throughout this book, I use examples of mundane but chronic traumatic events rather than dramatic, spectacular, and instantly life-changing events. Too often, we often assume that children who are chronically exposed to mundane toxic stress should be able to cope with it and will recover on their own.

Consider, for example, the 10-year-old who repeatedly comes to school with uncompleted homework because life at home is chaotic. If educators don't inquire into the child's life outside school, they may perceive and respond to uncompleted homework as willful defiance of classroom expectations. They may lecture the student that uncompleted homework will lead to poor performance in class. This student's brain and body will be flooded with stress hormones that evening when bedtime comes and the homework remains uncompleted, flooded again on the bus the next morning, flooded yet again walking through the school doors, and again and again each time the student thinks about being called out, yet again, for uncompleted homework.

This student is experiencing a chronic loss of psychological and emotional safety. We must think beyond spectacular and dramatic events to understand how chronic lack of support and care can be developmentally devastating.

Recovery Takes Time

We must remember that recovery from trauma takes time. We often forget this, even when the events are dramatic or spectacular.

Consider, for example, the way Chicago Public Schools responded to the tragic murder of 9-year-old Tyshawn Lee, who lived and attended school in the city's Auburn Gresham neighborhood. Tyshawn was playing in a park when a gunman lured him into a nearby alley and shot him because of his father's alleged gang ties. In response, Chicago Public Schools provided two weeks of crisis mental health support to students at Tyshawn's elementary school, hoping this would be enough to get students back to normal. After two weeks, students would be expected to self-regulate their behavior to meet school rules. It is likely that numerous students received punitive consequences for not being able to manage the dysregulation that results from living in a neighborhood with a fundamental lack of safety.

The Auburn Gresham community, located on Chicago's South Side, had experienced 838 violent crimes in the 365 days before Tyshawn's murder. What does "normal" mean when you grow up experiencing such a chronic loss of safety? What does self-regulation mean when your body is repeatedly flooded with stress hormones that activate your "fight, flight, or freeze" response?

Too Many Students Are Coping with Trauma

Traumatization and dysregulation are disproportionately likely among children who have or are experiencing the following conditions.

Homelessness. Children without stable housing are among the most invisible and vulnerable in our education system and have a high likelihood of stress-induced mental illness. Absence of stable housing results in a lack of basic needs being met, including access to food, healthcare, and transportation, and high mobility prevents the development of relationships and routines.

Chronic community violence. The unexpected and random nature of violence leads children to believe that the world is dangerous and others cannot be trusted. Overexposure to stress hormones can result in ongoing states of hypervigilance and hyperarousal, causing dysregulation.

Substance abuse. When parents abuse drugs or alcohol, children can be forced to take on caregiver responsibilities and provide for their own well-being. This can damage their ability to bond and can cause them to disregard social boundaries.

Domestic violence. Children exposed to domestic violence have a limited ability to focus due to chronic stress-induced hypervigilance. Shame may lead to suppressed emotional distress that may be expressed as aggressive and disruptive behaviors, whining and clinginess, or isolation and emotional withdrawal.

Caregiver separation. This can result from events such as incarceration and divorce, which can cause extreme changes to household structures and routines. The return of the separated caregiver can also increase stress if there is difficulty reestablishing the child–caregiver relationship, which can manifest as anxiety, guilt, distrust, and socioemotional withdrawal.

Caregiver deportation threat. Students whose caregivers face potential deportation are more likely than others to experience food and housing insecurity and have limited access to healthcare and other social services. The chronic activation of fear in their lives can cause severe anxiety, lead them to view the world as dangerous and uncertain, and cause them to have difficulty envisioning the future.

The Neurobiology of Trauma

It is critical for educators to keep in mind that our **primary response** to traumatic stressors is automatic and out of conscious control. We can, however, learn to bring these automatic responses under the **secondary control** of our self-regulation and logical reasoning systems. This secondary control is the central task of **socialization**—the process of shaping children's management of their instinctive thoughts, feelings, and behaviors so they align with sociocultural expectations. To do this, it is important to first understand how physiological and neurochemical responses to stress affect thinking, emotion, and behavior.

Neurobiology refers to the brain structures, the release of neurochemicals and hormones, and the neuron-firing patterns that determine how we process information, feel emotions, and behave in response to internal and external stimuli. Whenever trauma occurs, an individual's neurobiological system has been either temporarily or permanently altered, affecting brain development. Our brains develop from the bottom up, with higher, more complex functions building on the strength of lower, less complex functions. Therefore, if our lower, less complex functions are not well developed, we can become developmentally stuck at lower levels of maturity as we age.

Take for example, the 24-year-old who functions at the emotional level of an egocentric 8-year-old because they haven't healed from being traumatized by the terror of the police breaking down their door, arresting their parent (their primary source of emotional safety), and then being placed into foster care.

As traumatized individuals age, more complex functions can become destabilized because their precursors are not well established. Take, for example, the 35-year-old who flits from one life goal to the next because of a weak ability to sequentially order milestones and delay gratification. This inability to persist with self-identified goals may be due to chronically destabilizing financial, housing, and food insecurity that was experienced when young.

One Mind, Three Brains

Thinking of our minds as having three distinct component "brains" is a useful way of understanding both the effects of trauma and the ways we process information and experiences (Cantor, 2009). The survival, emotional, and thinking brains represent the three areas of the human brain shown in Figure 1.2. (This is a generalization, of course, as each

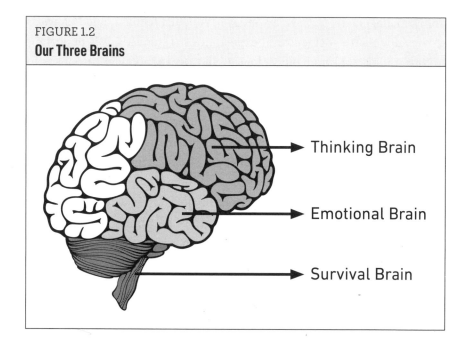

FIGURE 1.2
Our Three Brains

Thinking Brain

Emotional Brain

Survival Brain

"brain" is involved in numerous developmental systems and interacts with other brain structures and neurochemicals to determine any specific behavior.)

Almost everyone is born with a well-functioning **survival brain**, which is located just at the base of the human brain and includes the basal ganglia, brain stem, and other structures. The structures of the survival brain are much like those in the brains of reptiles and manage functions such as hunger, breathing, body temperature, and fear responses. Without conscious "thinking," the structures in the survival brain manage self-preservation and survival.

As we develop and mature, our **emotional brain**, which includes the amygdala, hippocampus, thalamus, and other structures, takes over our information-processing and decision-making functions. The structures of the limbic system that make up the emotional brain wrap around the survival brain and manage mood, memory, hormone control, and quick emotional judgments like good versus bad and safe versus threatening.

With continued maturation, safe and supportive developmental environments, and cognitive stimulation, the **thinking brain**, particularly the prefrontal cortex, begins to dominate, enabling strong impulse control and long-term planning. The neocortex and the other outermost structures of the brain are responsible for abstract and rational thought, reasoned decision making, and problem solving.

Under stress and threat, decision making is largely driven by the emotional brain—that is, by how we feel rather than by the facts of the situation. If the stress is prolonged or intense enough to cause a loss of feelings of safety, our survival brain takes over decision making, causing us to act instinctively.

The optimal situation is one in which our developing brains are protected from traumatic stressors that repeatedly activate our survival and emotional brains while regularly receiving supportive input to stimulate our thinking brain (National Scientific Council on the Developing Child, 2010). Over time, this allows us to develop the capacity to process and then modulate our instinctive and emotional reactions to stress. We learn to respond deliberately, moving from feeling an emotion to responding appropriately rather than rashly acting out.

For traumatized children, initially adaptive coping behaviors such as aggression, avoidance, paranoia, hypervigilance, and spacing out become maladaptive in contexts where no immediate harm is present. For example, a child who learns to dissociate during instances of sexual abuse may then respond in this way to all stressors, such as by withdrawing when called on in class to answer a difficult question (Perry, 2001).

Understanding Traumatic Triggers

For students coping with trauma, school can feel like a minefield of interpersonal interactions. Without warning, unexpected moments can trigger memories of a traumatic event that make them feel the need to protect themselves. When traumatic experiences remain unprocessed, the brain can be triggered to act as if the original threat is still present years after the incident occurred. Sometimes triggers are easy to identify and connect to a student's behavior, but educators are often left confused about what to do next. The student is often confused as well.

Over time, you may learn to identify a student's triggers by reflecting on the instances when emotional and behavioral changes occurred suddenly. If a student suddenly turns inward and becomes hard to reach, think about what was happening just before this shift.

Domains of Impairment

There are seven primary **domains of impairment** affecting children who have been exposed to toxic stress and trauma (see Figure 1.3) (Cook et al., 2005). Details of the trauma, such as the stage of development when it occurred, whether it is ongoing, and whether it was caused by a primary caregiver, determine the level of severity of impairment in each domain.

Domain 1: Brain and body. Repeated exposure to traumatic experiences interferes with the basic development and connections among neurons in the brain. Chronic exposure to traumatic stress also interferes

---

FIGURE 1.3
Domains of Impairment

Brain and Body Difficulty accessing rational thought in the face of over-whelming emotion	**Attachment** Withholding of emotions from others
Emotional Regulation Easy arousal and high-intensity emotional expression	**Behavior Regulation** Extremes of behavior, from overly confrontational to overly compliant
Dissociation Thoughts, emotions, and sensations that are discon-nected from awareness	**Thinking and Learning** Delays in learning, memory, reasoning, and attention
Self-Concept Sense of oneself as valued, worthy, and competent	

with the integration of left- and right-hemisphere brain functioning, making it hard for a child to access rational thought in the face of overwhelming emotion. Traumatized children are then inclined to react with extreme helplessness, confusion, withdrawal, or rage when stressed. They may also have a wide variety of medical problems, such as body pain, asthma, skin problems, autoimmune disorders, and psychogenic nonepileptic seizures.

Domain 2: Attachment. When children are placed in situations where they feel that they have to take responsibility for their own safety, particularly when their caregiver is the source of trauma, they attempt to exert some control by disconnecting from social relationships or by acting aggressively toward others. This may lead children to always be on the lookout for others who may threaten their safety and to withhold their feelings from others. These children often have great difficulty regulating their emotions, managing stress, having empathy for others, and using language to solve problems.

Domain 3: Emotional regulation. Children coping with trauma are easily aroused and express high-intensity emotions because of their low stress tolerance and high base anxiety level. They often feel out of control because of their inability to identify and name their internal emotional states of arousal (e.g., happy, sad, frightened). Because they have difficulty with both self-regulation and self-soothing, they may display chronic numbing of emotions, pervasive depressed mood, avoidance of negative and positive emotional situations, and maladaptive coping strategies.

Domain 4: Behavior regulation. Both under-controlled behaviors (such as aggressive or defiant behavior) and over-controlled behaviors (such as resistance to changes in routine) can develop as a way of coping with overwhelming stress and loss of safety. Children may appear to be self-destructive and aggressive toward others or, conversely, overly compliant.

Domain 5: Dissociation. Difficulty taking in and integrating information and experiences can cause children to have thoughts, emotions, and physical sensations that are disconnected from their conscious awareness. These children may self-soothe through repetitive behaviors without being conscious of doing so. Dissociation begins as a protective way to deal with overwhelming trauma, but over-reliance on it as a coping mechanism creates other self-regulation problems. Dissociation makes it hard for children to concentrate in the classroom and remember what was discussed.

Domain 6: Thinking and learning. Impairments in the domains listed above can cause traumatized children to exhibit significant delays in expressive and receptive language development, abstract reasoning, and problem solving; difficulty sustaining curiosity and attention; memory challenges due to distraction, misperception, and overwhelmed anxiety; and deficits in overall academic intelligence.

Domain 7: Self-concept. Children who have a safe and predictable environment and caregivers who are responsive and sensitive are able to develop a sense of themselves as valued, worthy, and competent. By contrast, traumatized children with impairments in the domains above can develop low self-esteem, feelings of shame and guilt, and a generalized sense of helplessness.

How Our Brain Protects Us from Harm

Our brain keeps us safe from harm by always maintaining at least a low level of vigilance for potential threats. The amygdala, which is a small, almond-shaped structure located deep in the middle of the temporal lobe (emotional brain), plays a central role in threat detection and activation of the "fight, flight, or freeze" response. Children growing up in a safe environment or with protective caregivers are able to maintain a low level of vigilance, minimizing anxiety and agitation and enabling them to focus their energy on learning and development.

Within fractions of a second of sensing danger, the survival brain and emotional brain trigger the release of neurochemicals that activate the sympathetic nervous system's "fight, flight, or freeze" response. Fractions of a second after that, the thinking brain begins to rationally assess the threat to determine whether the emotionally or instinctively driven response makes sense or if a different action would result in a better outcome. If the thinking brain determines that the threat is real, it stays out of the decision-making process so the individual can efficiently react based on instinct, habit, and past emotional learning. If it determines otherwise, however, it must engage in effortful self-regulation to override any instinctual action that has already been initiated. Traumatized children rarely get to this step of using their thinking brain to validate the legitimacy of the current threat.

The degree to which a student's survival brain and emotional brain perceive any particular stimulus as threatening will depend on their prior exposure to fear-inducing experiences. For example, some students might immediately throw a punch when a classmate accidentally bumps into them because of terrible previous experiences with physical bullying, whereas others might just utter a sarcastic "excuse me" and keep walking because their previous disputes have never risen above the level of mean looks.

Traumatized children need supportive adults who can, in the moment, act as their thinking brain to help them validate the objective nature of the threat and support their return to calm. Once the children are calmed, supportive adults need to help them rationally review and learn from the triggering experience so they can try to avoid overreacting in the future.

As we learn from our experiences, we all create and revise mental maps (memories) of danger and safety that include sights, sounds, and smells. These mental maps are stored in the hippocampus, which is part of a group of brain structures surrounding the survival brain. When the emotional brain triggers the alarm, the hippocampus compares what is happening in the current situation with existing mental maps of danger and safety. If, for example, it finds a strong association between a certain smell and a memory of harm, the individual can be sent into a state of fear and terror even when there are no objective signs of danger.

Because this processing occurs in the survival brain and emotional brain, children may not be able to cognitively connect the fear they are experiencing in the current moment to the previous traumatic experience. Instead, they experience an intense sense of fear, followed by a futile search for the current source of threat and then a desperate need to escape.

The survival brain and emotional brain do not distinguish between a triggered memory and the current moment, so they release neurochemicals to prepare for action before the thinking brain can rationally process the situation. It is not until these neurochemicals, which activate our "fight, flight, or freeze" response, begin to be reabsorbed that the thinking brain can rationally process the current situation.

Children can only learn to self-regulate their behavioral responses to triggering situations if they are supported by caring adults who

1. Recognize the signs and symptoms of trauma.
2. Provide a calming response.
3. Actively restore the children's sense of safety in the current context.
4. Help children cognitively process the experience so they can learn from it.

Let's revisit the traumatized student who throws a punch in response to being accidentally bumped by a classmate. For this student's behavior to improve, an educator standing nearby would need to

1. Deescalate the interaction.
2. Bring the student to a state of calm *before* attempting to discuss the behavior.
3. Review the interaction with both students to confirm that it was accidental and not motivated by the desire to cause harm.
4. Help the traumatized student understand they can lower their hypervigilance at school because there are caring adults around who will protect them.
5. Hold the student accountable with a restorative consequence, such as providing a brief and sincere apology to the other student.

When adults in the school can intervene with a developmentally supportive response each time a traumatized student reacts in a maladaptive way, that student will start to associate school with sanctuary and safety and their level of hypervigilance will decrease while they're in the building (Bloom, 1995).

Requirements for Meeting the Needs of Traumatized Students

To meet the developmental and educational needs of traumatized students, educators must do the following:

- Read and respond to children's emotional states as signaled by their behavior.
- Offer acceptance and warmth as well as accurate and appropriate feedback.
- Help children learn how to tolerate frustration during the learning process.
- Provide both boundaries for acceptable behavior and space for individual expression.

At the same time, educators must also learn to

- Manage feelings of frustration and irritation with students' off-task behaviors.

- Avoid responding to student behaviors with harsh or rejecting statements.
- Suppress any desire to emotionally withdraw from students exhibiting dysregulated behaviors.
- Recognize and attend to symptoms of secondary traumatic stress.
- Gauge their need to create emotional distance from students' traumas.

Figure 1.4 outlines some of the shifts educators must make to meet these requirements.

How Trauma Affects Classroom Learning

A student with trauma may feel compelled to swear at and push past an educator to escape feeling emotionally threatened by coursework that appears to be beyond their abilities. Such a student does not realize that what they are experiencing is an emotional threat based on the inaccurate

FIGURE 1.4

Shifts to Better Meet the Needs of Traumatized Students

Instead of...	Try...
Perceiving off-task behaviors in the framework of willful defiance	Perceiving off-task behaviors as cognitive, emotional, and behavioral dysregulation
Needing to place blame	Identifying the underlying cause of the problem
Perceiving challenging behaviors as a personal attack on authority	Perceiving off-task behaviors as signaling a need for behavioral support
Emphasizing culpability	Emphasizing reengagement
Engaging in punitive and escalating interactions	Engaging in redirection and deescalation
Denigrating students with verbal reprimands	Setting boundaries without showing emotion

perception that the educator is deliberately trying to embarrass them in front of the class. They don't consider that, by acting out, they have escalated the issue from uncompleted homework to verbal and physical assault. And they certainly don't consider the damage their behavior will cause to their relationship with the educator they depend upon for classroom learning. Furthermore, a student with a history of trauma is sensitized to move from embarrassment to shame to complete humiliation—that is, from low arousal to moderate arousal to high arousal—faster and in response to significantly less stress than a student who has had a history of caring developmental experiences (Perry, 2006).

Because students coping with trauma are often highly anxious, have low stress and frustration tolerance, and are fearful of shame and emotional harm, they are often reluctant to risk getting an answer wrong, attempt independent learning, or have their perspectives and understandings challenged. In such cases, students may

- Withdraw and dissociate, such as by sitting in silence, holding a glazed stare, or avoiding eye contact.
- Avoid and flee, such as by requesting frequent bathroom or water breaks, disturbing peers, or running out of the room.
- Fight back, such as by throwing a book across the room, responding to the educator's questions with profanity, or punching and kicking.

To learn in class, students must be able to selectively focus their attention on the relevant task, maintain that attention, organize their existing knowledge of the topic, manage anxiety in the face of learning challenges, and integrate the new content being presented with existing memories (Rosen & Hull, 2013). Traumatized students have trouble with these tasks because intrusive thoughts and a hyperactive stress-response system disrupt attention, control, and focus; create confusion; engender self-doubt; and impair information processing, all of which are serious obstacles to classroom learning.

Childhood trauma has been shown to negatively affect the "ABC+H" of school success: attendance, behavior, coursework, and health (Blodgett

& Lanigan, 2018). Students with three or more adverse childhood experiences are significantly more likely to have receptive and expressive language difficulties, be referred to special education, have lower standardized test scores, fail a grade, and be suspended or expelled (Grevstad, 2007).

Ensuring that students maintain cognitive and emotional states that facilitate learning is as important to their success as the quality of instruction. Educators must take a trauma responsive perspective to ensure that traumatized students experience learning opportunities as engagement opportunities and not as opportunities for failure (Perry, 2006). Unfortunately, an educator's intent to push their students' learning forward is often at odds with traumatized students' low frustration tolerance, as in the following examples:

- **Reading out loud:** Educator *intends* to engage students and make sure they're paying attention; the traumatized student *experiences* a risky proposition that could expose their lack of knowledge.
- **Writing on the board:** Educator *intends* this to be a chance for students to demonstrate skills; the traumatized student *experiences* the embarrassing prospect of revealing struggles with spelling to classmates.
- **Taking a pretest:** Educator *intends* to assess existing knowledge and identify learning needs; the traumatized student *experiences* a high-stakes evaluation of their intelligence, potential, and self-worth.

To improve these outcomes, we must gain a better understanding of the turbulence happening inside a child's brain and body and what it means for their behavioral functioning in educational contexts and their ability to benefit from rigorous instruction. By planning for how trauma affects children, educators can ensure that the challenges their students face outside school don't prevent them from succeeding in school.

Attending to Equity

Exposure to traumatic life events is not equally distributed, largely due to different levels of structural violence among different racial and ethnic communities (Cooper, 2007). According to the National Academies of

Science, Engineering, and Medicine (2017), structural violence is "the harm individuals, families, and communities experience from the economic and social structure, social institutions, and relations of power, privilege, and inequity that may harm people and communities by preventing them from getting their basic needs met." Structural violence can lead to "psychological injury resulting from protracted exposure to prolonged social and interpersonal trauma [without the resources to escape]" (National Academies of Sciences, Engineering, and Medicine, 2017, p. 21).

Access to school-based mental health supports is also not distributed evenly, and the children who need it most often receive the least support (Ridgard et al., 2015). This means that schools serving racial and ethnic minority and lower-income students are at risk for institutional collapse. One student's aggressive or emotional outburst can trigger the trauma of another student and amplify negative effects that ripple throughout the whole school community. Consequently, maintaining a positive school climate and culture is extremely difficult when large numbers of children coping with trauma and violence are concentrated in a given school (West et al., 2014).

Despite these challenges, schools are uniquely positioned to provide traumatized students with interpersonal rehabilitation (Chafouleas et al., 2016; Storch & Crisp, 2004). Schools that attend to students' social and emotional development in concert with their academic development and provide access to mental health supports at school (1) reduce the stigma that often causes people to shy away from mental health treatment and (2) eliminate the major obstacle of getting children to appointments during the day while parents are at work.

Because behavioral dysregulation is often perceived through the lens of disobedience, traumatized children face more discipline and behavior management than their peers, which can result in increased exclusion from classroom instruction. However, punitive and exclusionary discipline doesn't help matters—in fact, it is associated with even greater behavioral challenges and negative adult outcomes (Fabelo et al., 2011). This is because punitive and exclusionary discipline does not address the core issues underlying the student's behavior—and when students are excluded from school, they often feel an even greater sense of alienation upon their return.

Strong racial bias in the perception of dysregulated behaviors places Black children at the greatest risk of exclusionary punishments, even though evidence shows that Black students do not misbehave at higher rates than other students (Skiba et al., 2011). There also appears to be a broader schoolwide association between race and punitive discipline, such that even after accounting for a host of factors, including students' actual rates of disciplinary infractions, schools with higher proportions of Black students are significantly more likely to utilize punitive and exclusionary discipline (Welch & Payne, 2010). Specifically, Black students are more likely than White students to experience punitive and exclusionary discipline even after accounting for level of misbehavior or delinquency, academic performance, parental attention, school organization, economic disadvantage, drug use, educator victimization, and educator perceptions of lack of safety.

Trauma responsive educational practices help advance racial justice in education by adjusting the lens through which educators interpret dysregulated behavior and providing a toolbox of developmentally supportive responses. These intentional responses are grounded in research that identifies how schools serving mostly minority students effectively resist using punitive and exclusionary discipline (Hambacher, 2018).

Educators who use their power to promote racial justice

- Perceive themselves as advocates of educational standards for historically marginalized students.
- Gather information about students' lives outside school to understand the stressors they carry with them into the classroom.
- Build positive relationships with students that they then leverage to help students cultivate self-control and comply with policies and procedures.
- Proactively provide behavioral supports based on students' patterns of off-task behaviors.

- Utilize assets from students' cultures to facilitate engagement in learning.
- Provide a range of response opportunities so all students can experience success and mastery in the classroom.
- Understand that ensuring success for the most vulnerable does not harm, and often helps, all other students in the school.

Clarifying Misconceptions

Trauma responsive educators do not believe that *all* behavioral challenges are due to trauma. Many students act out to attract attention, to avoid schoolwork they find difficult, or out of plain old boredom. However, when consistent classroom management and engaged teaching practices are not enough, educators should look for symptoms of trauma as a causal factor in students' dysregulated behavior.

Being responsive to trauma does not mean reducing academic expectations for students. That would send the message that the educator has given up on the student and only lower the student's self-image. Instead, trauma responsive educators help students meet high expectations by taking into account their life circumstances and offering them multiple chances to demonstrate mastery.

Although we must be mindful of the need to meet students where they are, we must also acknowledge that children have tremendous abilities to adapt and change. With the right developmental supports, the harms caused by trauma can be overcome and post-traumatic growth is possible. For this to happen, educators must understand how students are affected by trauma and have access to training on the educational practices that can foster recovery and resilience.

2

Stress Prevention and Management for Educators

The COVID-19 pandemic brought renewed attention to issues of educator stress, burnout, and self-care. The sudden shift to remote learning for millions of families made parents intimately aware of the emotional labor that goes into educating children. Suddenly, secondary traumatic stress was being discussed as an issue central to education. We could no longer deny the importance of educators' emotional health in enabling them to support children affected by trauma (Cooper & Travers, 2012; Figley, 1995). Educators cannot be expected to show up and support high-needs students day after day without knowing that they themselves are supported as well.

Caring educator–student relationships enable learning to flourish and are among the most powerful tools for promoting recovery from traumatic experiences. However, the stronger the educator–student relationship, the more the educator risks being negatively affected by being trauma adjacent. Even though you haven't directly experienced the traumatic event, you are *personally touched* by hearing about and helping students' process tragic events and experiences.

Feelings of anxiety and emotional distress, mental or emotional burnout, and being overwhelmed by students' traumas are not signs of personal weakness (Koenig et al., 2019). Rather, they are simply the price we pay for caring about those more vulnerable than ourselves. In this chapter, you'll learn about some ways to prevent, manage, and heal from the psychologically, emotionally, and physically demanding job of caring for children and youth.

Like many educators, it's possible you are so focused on meeting your students' needs that you don't notice your own needs. However, you cannot give your students compassion if you can't give it to yourself—at least not for very long.

The negative effects of professional stress ripple out and are detrimental for all. For educators, high levels of stress can cause emotional exhaustion; social detachment; heightened senses of fear, anxiety, and helplessness; and feelings of estrangement from work. They can also disrupt how educators process and respond to interactions with students, colleagues, and others. Emotionally unhealthy educators are less perceptive of and responsive to students' needs and less able to provide engaging instruction. Further, educator burnout has severe consequences for the broader system, as high turnover contributes to significant declines in student achievement, loss of investment in staff training, and destabilization of school culture.

The Burnout Process

Developing knowledge and awareness of how stress works is the first step to mitigating and managing its negative effects. As Figure 2.1 shows, the high rate of burnout in schools with a lot of traumatized students is the

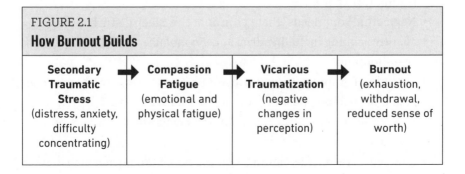

FIGURE 2.1
How Burnout Builds

| Secondary Traumatic Stress (distress, anxiety, difficulty concentrating) | Compassion Fatigue (emotional and physical fatigue) | Vicarious Traumatization (negative changes in perception) | Burnout (exhaustion, withdrawal, reduced sense of worth) |

end of a process that builds gradually over stages: secondary traumatic stress, compassion fatigue, vicarious traumatization, and burnout.

Vicarious trauma and secondary traumatic stress may develop immediately, whereas compassion fatigue often builds up over time. All three will lead to burnout without some form of intervention to reduce exposure to stress and provide coping supports. Every stage can negatively affect educators' effectiveness in the classroom, often without them realizing it (Butler et al., 2017).

Secondary Traumatic Stress

Secondary traumatic stress is the result of bearing witness (directly or indirectly) to another's trauma. It is normal to worry about whether your students' basic needs are being met. Without help processing difficult information, listening to their stories can constrain your capacity as an educator and impact your functioning in other areas of your life. It can manifest in outward behaviors such as irritability, angry outbursts, or having difficulty breathing. It can also manifest as intrusive thoughts, memories or nightmares related to students' experiences, or insomnia.

Learning about the traumatic experiences of students, feeling empathetic toward them, and being limited in your ability to change the conditions in which they live is undeniably stressful. The more you understand the following signs and symptoms of secondary traumatic stress, the better you will be able to manage or even prevent them:

- A heightened sense of empathy: being easily triggered by a student's traumatic experience.
- Neglecting your needs: changes in appetite, sleep disturbances, maladaptive coping including drug and alcohol use, gambling, or excessive shopping.
- Feelings of grandiosity: believing that you are the only one who can help a student and pushing yourself too hard to do so.
- Low sense of self-efficacy: an inability to tackle daily responsibilities in and out of the classroom.
- Low self-esteem: questioning your purpose and the meaning of life.

- Difficulty concentrating: decreased ability to focus on the task at hand or make decisions.
- Isolating from others: consciously or unconsciously detaching from your students and your loved ones.

Compassion Fatigue

Compassion fatigue is a kind of emotional exhaustion that leads people working in caring professions to deplete their reserves of sympathy for others (Coetzee & Klopper, 2010). This stage is reached after prolonged and intense exposure to distress. Educators experiencing compassion fatigue may become dispirited and increasingly cynical at work or act disrespectfully toward students and colleagues. The degree to which compassion fatigue affects an educator's work may ebb and flow from one day to the next, but often it just gets increasingly worse. Here are some of the symptoms of compassion fatigue:

- A change in attitude toward work: loss of confidence in students' abilities, irritability with colleagues, negative thoughts about aspects of work that you used to enjoy.
- Changes in daily routines.
- Significant decrease or increase in appetite.
- Distancing yourself from spiritual or emotional supports.
- Increased reliance on substances.
- Symptoms of depression: feelings of apathy or agitation, extreme sadness or excessive crying, loss of interest in hobbies, repetitive negative thoughts (particularly about work).

Vicarious Trauma

Vicarious trauma is a decline in psychological well-being from exposure to someone else's experiences with trauma. Symptoms may include anxiety, depression, and paranoia; a perception of the world as unsafe and uncontrollable; and changes in spiritual beliefs. Vicarious trauma occurs when educators are not equipped with effective coping strategies or when they've exhausted existing coping strategies. Addressing vicarious trauma requires an awareness of one's well-being and an ability to recognize when one needs professional support (Cavanaugh, 2016). Here are some of the symptoms of vicarious trauma:

- Hypervigilance: heightened or constant feelings of alertness, always on the lookout for dangers or threats inside and outside work.
- Poor boundaries: taking work very personally and attempting to control events, difficulty empathizing or overempathizing.
- Avoidance: disconnecting and shutting down from work to cope with stress, feeling emotionally severed from work.
- Addictions: using distractions of any kind to "check out."
- Chronic exhaustion and physical ailments: fatigue or aches/pains of any kind beyond the ordinary.
- Minimizing: diminishing experiences through egregious comparisons.
- Coping with intense feelings through cynicism or anger.

Burnout

Finally, burnout is a state of physical, emotional, psychological, and spiritual exhaustion due to job strain coupled with frustration and a sense of powerlessness. Burnout is associated with negative attitudes and behaviors toward work, and it can manifest as increased absenteeism, declining job performance, and reduced physical and mental health (Ross et al., 2012). For educators, burnout also shows up as a decrease in frustration tolerance and the ability to positively respond to dysregulated student behaviors. This decrease in tolerance and professional efficacy erodes positive relationships with students and colleagues and further exacerbates stress. Here are some of the symptoms of burnout:

- Exhaustion: feeling emotionally drained because your efforts are going unnoticed/unrecognized, increased fatigue and desire for sleep.
- Depersonalization: distancing yourself from students and colleagues and having callous thoughts about them.

- Diminished feelings of professional accomplishment: feeling like no matter what you do, your efforts are not enough, your professional efficacy is declining, and pressure and demands at work are unbearable.
- Feelings of professional inadequacy: a growing sense of insecurity in work performance, uncertainty, and second-guessing decisions at work.

Reflecting on the Burnout Process

Take a moment to reflect on each stage of the burnout process by answering the following questions:

- **Secondary traumatic stress:** Do you feel exhausted and a little panicked on Monday mornings when you think about going back into the classroom?
- **Compassion fatigue:** Do you refrain from learning about your students' lives because it has become emotionally draining to hear about problems that you can't control?
- **Vicarious traumatization:** Are you always on the lookout for potential threats in and out of the classroom? Does it feel like you're always looking out for the next troubling incident?
- **Burnout:** Do you regularly think about leaving your job but stay year after year only because it feels like it would be too hard to change careers?

High levels of stress and secondary traumatic stress in the first year of teaching are enough to cause some educators to leave the profession. Others persist for several years and then depart soon after reaching the burnout stage. Some experience burnout within five years; for others it takes fifteen (Borman & Dowling, 2008; Rinke, 2007). Whatever the case, too many educators continue teaching long after losing their ability to effectively meet students' needs.

ferent levels of burnout risk. You are at increased risk if

ıany students who have or are experiencing trauma.

- ı̣ ᴌosely connected to a student who is coping with traumatic events.
- A student has shared intense stories of their experience with trauma.
- You have a heightened sensitivity to the needs of others.
- You have personally experienced trauma and have not received adequate support for dealing with it.
- You tend to neglect or lack awareness of your own social and emotional needs.
- You tend to try to do everything on your own and regularly push too hard.

The Seven Domains of Well-being

Being prepared to overcome life's challenges means supporting each of the seven domains of well-being: physical, psychological, cognitive, social, financial, spiritual, and environmental (Hydon et al., 2015). These interconnected domains determine how you navigate relationships, cope with challenges, and handle responsibilities in your professional and personal life. As you consider each of these seven domains and their associated support strategies, keep in mind your strengths and weaknesses in each will be different from someone else's, and your approach to self-care must be authentic to who you are, your specific needs, and your sources of support:

1. **Physical well-being** includes
   - Eating healthy, balanced meals on a regular schedule.
   - Getting six to eight hours of sleep.
   - Taking care of your body and exercising regularly.
   - Using healthcare services.
2. **Psychological well-being** includes
   - Having a sense of purpose.
   - Maintaining high self-esteem.
   - Taking a strengths-based approach to challenges.

— Asking for help when needed.

— Cultivating emotional awareness.

— Keeping a sense of humor.

— Communicating thoughts and feelings.

3. **Cognitive well-being** includes

— Engaging in activities that promote intellectual, social, and cultural growth as well as curiosity and identity development.

— Participating in learning communities and hobbies that promote creative expression and bring joy and fulfillment.

4. **Social well-being** includes

— Nurturing supportive relationships with colleagues, family, friends, and others.

— Surrounding yourself with positive influences.

— Having a sense of belonging and connection to others, cultures, and community.

— Developing and maintaining trusting relationships.

5. **Financial well-being** includes

— Providing for the basic necessities of life.

— Having the capacity to absorb financial shock.

— Meeting financial goals.

— Having the freedom to make financial choices.

— Being able to afford leisure activities.

6. **Spiritual well-being** includes

— Connecting to a higher power.

— Reflecting on your purpose.

— Participating in religious services or groups.

— Seeking to further develop your spirituality.

7. **Environmental well-being** includes

— Taking a walk outdoors.

— Camping.

— Gardening.

— Being outside.

— Contributing to an environmental cause.

Attending to Equity by Acknowledging How Educators of Color Are Affected by a Racially Inequitable System

Educators who are members of racial or ethnic minority groups often work in schools that are culturally triggering and lacking in supports to help them manage race-related stressors at work (Terada, 2021). There is a popular misperception that racial microaggressions, while offensive, cause no real harm, but research shows that the negative impact of racial microaggressions is profound and suggests that subtle microaggressions may have the strongest effects (Sue, 2010). As one group of researchers stated: "The stress of one racial microaggression can last long after the assault because the victim often continues to spend time with the micro-aggressor while considering whether the assailant intended harm, and whether or how they must launch a sufficient response" (Yosso et al., 2009, p. 670).

Because many educators of color work in schools where they are the only or among only a few non-White faculty, they can end up shouldering the burden of carrying the diversity, equity, and inclusion work in contexts where there is limited reward for that work. For this reason, among others, Black and Latinx educators are significantly more likely to leave the profession than their White counterparts (Carr, 2022). If you are an educator of color, you need to take a close look at race-related workplace stressors and prioritize self-care to counteract them. The allyship of White educators is vital as well, both to show solidarity and to help shoulder the burden of advocating for marginalized students.

Compassionate self-care is critical for the professional longevity of educators of color. This includes clearly identifying personal boundaries and communicating them to colleagues. You are no good to the students you fight for if you wear yourself down so much that you can't extend compassion to and advocate for them when they need it most. Boundary setting is a process of continuous self-reflection and negotiating the balance between your own expectations and those of others. Take moments to pause, breathe deeply, critically reflect, and ask yourself: *What aspects of my work are draining me and do I need to do less of?* Then, pause a little longer, breathe even more deeply, critically reflect, and ask yourself: *What aspects of my work are energizing me and do I need to do more of?*

We are in a historical period during which it is professionally risky to teach accurate and truthful Black history. In this political climate, it takes a tremendous amount of cognitive and emotional energy to teach for the purposes of resistance to, transgression of, and liberation from racial oppression. To educate in the midst of fear, you must ensure that some of the work that you do energizes you and fills you with joy. These positive professional moments are necessary if you are to engage in the many uncomfortable conversations that push forward educational equity and justice.

Educators of color, I encourage you to be both brave and bold in recognizing that, although you may not be able to be fully yourself at work, you can still integrate a broad array of diverse cultural references into the work that you do. Fighting back against injustice doesn't have to cost you your livelihood; resistance comes in many forms, including that of rediscovering your joy and passion in the cultural components of your practice.

Center yourself by sharing with your students the unique contributions you bring to your school and classroom as an educator of color. Add cultural diversity to the artwork that decorates your classroom or office; broaden the range of learning materials and options that students can choose from for projects. Find, take, and make opportunities to incorporate non-White and transnational references, both historical and contemporary, into your daily work. Supplement the curriculum you are given to honor historically marginalized cultures. When you take these actions, you are giving yourself small daily doses of cultural validation.

Guidelines for Self-Care

Self-care is about taking deliberate action to improve or restore health and well-being, and it is therefore a powerful tool for preventing, managing, and recovering from intense stressors (Beltman et al., 2011; Hydon et al., 2015; Klusmann et al., 2008). Follow these broad guidelines as you engage in self-care across the seven domains of well-being:

- Recognize and accept that you cannot meet all your students' needs.
- Establish healthy boundaries between work and home.
- Seek and accept professional support (instructional coaching, professional development) and personal support (a sympathetic ear, social time with friends).
- Put your body's basic needs first and establish healthy sleep, exercise, diet, and leisure conditions.
- Use your employee benefits to seek and receive physical and mental health care.

Claiming Time for Self-Care

Time is fluid; we make time for the experiences that we prioritize. Failing to engage in self-care is less about not having enough time for it than about whether you prioritize it. My work with educators has taught me that many perceive it to be a little bit selfish or consider it an either/or proposition: either you prioritize self-care or you meet your students' needs. This is a dangerous misperception. In fact, self-care increases the likelihood that you can meet their needs.

Self-care is fundamentally about your intentional efforts to maintain wellness and wholeness in ways that are authentic for you. Aim to develop sustainable practices that you can integrate into your daily life to meaningfully improve your well-being. It won't be easy, but it can be simple, and though it will require intentional effort, it won't be overwhelming.

Integrate Self-Care into Your Workday

Self-care asks that you respect your emotional, financial, and physical needs; nurture relationships at work and outside it; and maintain balance and boundaries between work and your personal life. This will be most sustainable when you can integrate self-care into your workday as well as your personal time. Here are a few suggestions for doing this:

- **Take a whole-class break for mindful stretching.** When you feel a high level of tension in your body or on edge emotionally, this strategy can provide a much-needed emotional reset for both you and your students. Being fully present and aware of your mood lets you develop the capacity to recognize and choose how to respond to stressful situations. A quick online search for "mindful stretching" will turn up many brief videos that you can use.
- **Take a whole-class break for collaborative problem solving.** When you feel overwhelmed by students pulling you in multiple directions and competing for your attention, share these difficulties with the class (without calling any students out by name) and collectively discuss how to improve the situation.
- **Put *yourself* on your daily schedule.** If you regularly feel drained by the end of the day or feel like you never have a moment to yourself, make self-care time visible for yourself, your students, and your colleagues. Consider laminating a sign for your door that says, "Please do not disturb. Self-care in progress." When you do this, you reaffirm to yourself and to others that time to recharge is a necessary part of giving of yourself to others.

Mindful Self-Care

Mindful self-care is a truly transformative everyday practice. Research shows that mindfulness is an effective and sustainable strategy for buffering against compassion fatigue and burnout (Lomas et al., 2017).

I define mindful self-care as engaging in a variety of brief mindfulness practices that focus on using your breath to pause and center yourself in the present moment, pushing out regrets of the past and worries of the future.

Try it: For a moment—lasting the length of just one deep breath or maybe a full minute—allow yourself to nonjudgmentally connect with your thoughts, your emotions, and your body. You don't need a special space to do this. You can ground yourself in the present moment wherever you are. You can do this while sitting at your desk. You can get up and walk around, taking deep breaths with each slow step. You can stand still or stretch.

Over time, regular engagement with brief moments of mindfulness can increase your ability to regulate your emotions and tolerate distress. Mindfulness extends your ability to nonjudgmentally move through the many professional and personal frustrations you experience each day. Don't relegate self-care to something you will get to only after your work is done; take time throughout the day to engage in it.

To start practicing mindful self-care, consider taking the following steps:

- **Set aside some time to begin.** All you need are a few moments of time and some space—it doesn't even need to be a quiet space. You just need to quiet *yourself* in whatever space you are in.
- **Observe the present moment.** Perceive your thoughts, feelings, and bodily sensations. You are not trying to achieve a state of meditative calm. You are simply paying attention to and accepting the present moment for what it is.
- **Notice and release your judgments.** Accept all your thoughts, feelings, and sensations as being neither good nor bad, but simply part of your human experience.
- **Actively engage in self-compassion.** Don't judge your wandering mind. Instead, whenever you notice it wandering, gently return it to the present moment.

From Self-Care to Collective Care

Becoming more attuned to your needs and engaging in self-care are critical to improved well-being, but professional stress is best prevented and managed with the support of your colleagues (Skaalvik & Skaalvik, 2015). Research shows that collegial social support provides significant protection against high levels of stress (Klassen, 2010). The climate of the school is important not only for student success but also for the well-being and efficacy of educators (Eldor & Shoshani, 2016).

Educator stress is part reality (large class size, diverse student and parent needs, classroom management challenges, testing pressures, accountability demands) and part perception (feeling frustrated and anxious about one's reality) (Abel & Sewell, 1999; Kokkinos, 2007). When stressors accumulate, physical and emotional exhaustion ensues (Skaalvik & Skaalvik, 2015).

The five major categories of educator stress are as follows:

- **Organizational structure.** Higher levels of educator stress are found in schools without a supportive culture, a collaborative and collegial environment, trust among colleagues, and strong principal leadership.
- **Job demands.** The stress of meeting students' complex needs is often exacerbated by a constantly increasing workload, high-stakes testing, and other accountability pressures that threaten educators' jobs.
- **Professional development.** Educators often cite a lack of knowledge about managing emotional and behavioral issues as a primary source of stress.
- **Support and autonomy.** Stress is commonly found in schools without adequate professional support, structured opportunities for meaningful decision making, and low levels of autonomy for educators.

Investing in Educator Well-Being

Administrators at the state, district, and school levels must help educators develop the tools and skills and create the educational context necessary to meet students' needs in ways that do not undermine anyone's well-being (Hydon et al., 2015). Many educators, particularly those in underresourced urban and rural schools, work in a system that forces them to push their human capacity to the limits, negatively affecting their well-being. Because this problem is systemic, the most effective remedy is collective care. Following are some ways states, districts, and schools can collectively address systemic stressors in education.

Policies and practices. Schools can and should adjust their policies and practices in ways that reduce or prevent stress, increase job satisfaction, and strengthen staff resiliency, such as by

- Fostering a participatory and collaborative work environment.
- Maintaining open communication.
- Developing peer and administrative supports.
- Encouraging professional growth.
- Including educators in meaningful decision-making processes.
- Identifying educators who are especially susceptible to stress and providing them with formal mentoring programs.

Professional development. Well-chosen professional development focused on advancing educators' classroom management skills is one of the best investments administrators can make to reduce educator stress. Lack of adequate classroom management skills can be an enormous stressor (Dicke et al., 2014). Fortunately, hands-on professional development has been shown to improve educators' self-efficacy in the classroom, helping them create the context necessary for students to benefit from rigorous instruction (Aloe et al., 2014; Brouwers & Tomic, 2000; Dicke et al., 2014; Zee & Kooman, 2016).

Reassurance of worth. When administrators regularly reassure educators of their worth, they are less likely to suffer burnout (Russell et al., 1987). Principals can proactively reduce the chances of burnout by visiting more classrooms both to acknowledge educator's skills and abilities and to provide supportive, skill-building feedback.

Safe spaces. Like the students they serve, educators need their own safe spaces for sharing about and healing from secondary trauma. Discussions with peers in these spaces help make clear that stress is not a personal weakness while also reducing professional isolation and building networks of support. Administrators and educators can even establish formal healing circles to cultivate a culture of mutual care and aid.

Workplace health and wellness promotion programs. These kinds of programs create work-based opportunities and incentives for exercise and healthy eating. They are well worth the investment, including the cost for an extra hour of staff time (either bimonthly or quarterly) to engage in a wellness activity. Here are a few ways to promote health and wellness in the workplace:

- When possible, turn staff meetings into outdoor walking meetings.
- Provide friendly competitive incentives for exercising or eating healthy.
- Have a wellness coach teach an afterschool seminar.
- Compensate a staff member for teaching a fitness class before or after school.

Institutionalized social and emotional learning. It is important to make social and emotional learning a focus because behavioral challenges related to poor student self-regulation are the largest professional stressor reported by educators (Beltman et al., 2011). Schools with social and emotional learning programs tend to have lower rates of staff anxiety and depression, higher quality student–educator interactions, more educator engagement, and greater perceived educator control (Jennings & Greenberg, 2009). For example, educators in schools that implement schoolwide positive behavioral interventions and supports (SWPBIS) have lower levels of burnout as well as higher levels of self-efficacy (Jennings & Greenberg, 2009). In the most effective SWPBIS models, educators receive ongoing coaching that helps them improve the quality of interactions with students.

Identifying systemic ways of attending to educator health and well-being must be a fundamental aspect of any educational system. Even the most resource-challenged schools can implement policies and practices that reduce educator stress. I encourage you to talk with your colleagues, share what you have learned, and work toward implementing collective care. Start with a few committed colleagues, then invite all to join in and institutionalize collective care as part of your school's culture.

3

Mindfulness for Well-Being and Professional Longevity

Mindfulness is a practice that can be implemented schoolwide to improve outcomes for both educators and students. By building brief moments of dedicated time for mindfulness practices into the school day, educators and students strengthen their ability to respond in thoughtful ways rather than reacting out of stress and anxiety. This is because mindfulness builds cognitive and emotional self-regulation and, by doing so, also builds behavioral self-regulation (Princing, 2018).

Mindfulness involves cultivating an awareness of yourself by purposefully paying attention to the present moment and being aware of where you are, how you're feeling, and what you're doing (Siegel et al., 2016). It is also about building your capacity to nonjudgmentally allow thoughts, experiences, and emotions to unfold (Davidson et al., 2003). As you train your mind to restore your inner self, the weight of problems lightens and you are better able to solve problems because you can perceive the present more clearly (Smith & Jelen, 2016).

The intentional practice of focusing on the present moment as it unfolds without judgment can create long-lasting alterations in the structure and function of the parts of the brain that are responsible for cognitive, emotional, and behavioral regulation (Siegel et al., 2016). The following mindful traits will begin to occur without conscious intention or effort:

- **Acting with awareness:** being aware of what you are doing while you are doing it.
- **Being nonjudgmental:** accepting experiences and emotional reactions to experiences without judging yourself for having them.
- **Being nonreactive:** being able to return to a state of emotional equilibrium and neutrality during and after stressful events.
- **Being aware of internal emotions:** engaging with the full range of positive and negative emotions and being able to describe your internal world.

These ways of being become instinctive traits because the practice of mindfulness stimulates neurons and induces changes in areas of the brain associated with attention regulation, learning and memory, emotion regulation, impulse control, and empathy (Hölzel, Lazar, et al., 2011; Siegel, 2007). Changes include the following:

- Increased concentration of gray matter in regions of the brain involved in learning and memory processing, emotion regulation, self-referential processing, and perspective taking (Hölzel, Carmody, et al., 2011).
- Increased ability to maintain present-moment attention despite external distractions, unpleasant events, and mentally taxing tasks (Hölzel, Lazar, et al., 2011).
- Decreased physiological reactivity, rumination, and fluctuation of mood states (Hölzel, Lazar, et al., 2011; Jha et al., 2010; Opialla et al., 2015).

Mindfulness is not the suppression of negative or distressing emotions like sadness, anger, or anxiety. Rather, it facilitates your ability to take informed action in response to stress. Mindfulness is also not the simple, passive acceptance of circumstances—only of the preset moment. Learning mindfulness is most effective when you are calm and when you use it for purposes other than stress management.

Mindfulness as a Coping Strategy

Research shows that the chronic activation of negative emotions by challenging interactions with others is particularly damaging for educator well-being, leading to compassion fatigue and withdrawal (Chang, 2009; Evers et al., 2004). The emotional and behavioral dysregulation displayed by children who are coping with trauma can make it challenging for the adults around them to maintain their own self-regulation. Thankfully, mindfulness is an adaptive coping strategy that has been shown to transform the ways educators respond to these daily workplace stressors.

Mindfulness encourages you to

- Reflect on your interpretations of stressful interactions with students, which in turn helps you learn from past interactions to plan for future challenges.
- See off-task behaviors as providing helpful information about students' emotional and psychological functioning, which in turn helps you remain emotionally neutral.
- View students' behavioral mistakes as part of the learning process for which nobody is to blame.
- Think of stressful interactions with students as learning challenges rather than personal threats, thereby reducing the likelihood of emotional reactivity.
- Face rather than avoid distressing thoughts, emotions, and interactions, creating opportunities to engage with and learn from challenging interactions.
- Maintain a composed awareness of your emotions, reducing the likelihood that suppressed emotions will determine decision making.

Research has shown that practicing mindfulness helps educators to

- Sense when a negative emotion begins to form.
- Notice effects of the emotion, such as a tightness of the chest or heat rising to the cheeks.
- Feel and recognize, without judging, the situation that brought on the negative emotion (Singh et al., 2013).

Mindfulness in Action

Let's take a closer look at how mindfulness works. Imagine yourself solving a math equation on the board while becoming increasingly agitated as two students persist in talking. Don't ignore the students and suppress the negative emotions that arise; instead, by allowing yourself to pause and be fully aware of how you are feeling in the present moment without judging your emotions, you are better able to catch yourself from reacting out of frustration and punitively and publicly calling out the students. Pause and take a few deep breaths while still facing the board. Then complete the equation, turn around, and give the students a hand signal to stop talking. Later, pull them aside for a quiet discussion. This kind of mindful response allows you to continue the lesson, communicate your classroom management requests, and maintain the dignity of the students who need more behavioral support.

Using Mindfulness to Identify and Manage Triggers

Mindful self-understanding—your ability to recognize and identify your triggers and emotional response patterns—is the first step to proactively managing the stress and secondary trauma that can result from the emotional labor of meeting traumatized students' developmental needs. What's more, mindfully understanding yourself increases your ability to be responsive instead of reactive in how you engage with both students and colleagues.

Making space and time for mindfulness in schools can also help move staff and students from being reactive to being responsive when stressful situations arise. Educators are reactive when their actions are determined by emotions triggered by student behaviors. When this occurs, the reaction is often much more intense and punitive than is warranted by the immediate situation. By contrast, educators are responsive when they separate their triggered emotions from the developmentally supportive responses they display to students. The focus here is on utilizing pedagogical practices that help students build their coping and self-regulation skills.

When Educators Have Trauma of Their Own

When educators have an emotional or behavioral response to student actions that are much more intense or punitive than is warranted by the immediate situation, it may be because they have trauma of their own that has been triggered by the student's actions.

For some educators, having coped with toxic stress and trauma may even be the reason they entered the profession, and it may be what enables them to be empathetic to students' needs. However, those sensitivities also put these educators at risk of being triggered. This often happens without warning, when educators suddenly learn about a student who has trauma similar to their own. In some cases, educators may become defensive and distance themselves from such students in an unconscious effort to protect their mental health. This can leave educators with limited psychological and emotional resources for meeting the student's needs.

Educators can also be triggered by events and experiences that remind them of past or current job-related stressors, worries, and anxieties. For example, some student behaviors trigger educators' anxieties about being disrespected and losing control of the classroom. Educators must remember to respond to off-task behaviors with inquiries into the student's needs, redirection, and opportunities for self-correction.

Student eye rolling is one common trigger for educators, many of whom believe that it communicates disrespect. But educators who respond to eye rolling with anger, resentment, and punishment are not responding to the severity of the immediate behavior; rather, they are reacting to some previous experience that makes them anticipate behavioral escalation.

Inserting a one- to three-breath mindful pause when you sense that you have been triggered by a student's behavior can strengthen your ability to make measured decisions and provide logical rather than threatening consequences. Students will perceive you as less emotionally volatile and as holding high academic and behavioral expectations that are supportive, not punitive. The result is that both educators and students have more of their cognitive and emotional capacities freed up for instruction and learning (Skinner & Beers, 2016). (See Figure 3.1 for more benefits of mindfully responding to triggers.)

FIGURE 3.1
Benefits of Mindfully Responding to Triggers

Mindfulness enables educators to . . .	Then students experience educators as . . .
Be measured and emotionally calm in response to dysregulated student behaviors.	Less nervous, irritable, and easily set off.
Make disciplinary decisions based on facts of the current situation rather than emotion or student reputation.	Fully present rather than pulling in baggage from past challenging interactions.
Show an increased willingness to stay engaged in a challenging interaction and open to their own and students' emotions and experiences.	Responsive listeners who are open to hearing students' perspectives.
Let go of negative emotions swiftly after challenging interactions.	Returning to learning swiftly after challenging interactions.
Be more likely to feel and express positive emotions toward teaching and students.	Enjoying teaching and classroom learning as engaging and fun.

Attending to Equity by Using Mindfulness to Increase Cultural Humility

Mindful reflection practices can help you to intentionally reframe and reinterpret your students' verbal and nonverbal communication through a lens of nonjudgmental understanding. The aim is to get into the habit of reflecting on experiences and interactions with students and their families to identify whether your cultural lens may be imposing incorrect assumptions about their motivations and values.

This is about going beyond surface behaviors to identify some of the potential what-ifs in students' lives that could explain (not excuse) maladaptive behaviors. Only by understanding the underlying causes can you help them learn to engage in the behaviors that are associated with success at school. Before undertaking the reflection exercise that follows, consider the set of what-ifs in Figure 3.2 for a student who frequently talks out of turn and reacts aggressively to small frustrations.

The mindful reflection detailed below was developed for a school that served a mostly minority student body but had only a handful of non-White educators. Staff often struggled with students and their families that they perceived as not valuing education or disrespecting the school community. They also regularly found themselves navigating communication breakdowns when students and families were offended and upset by staff members' earnest attempts to help.

FIGURE 3.2
Sample What-Ifs

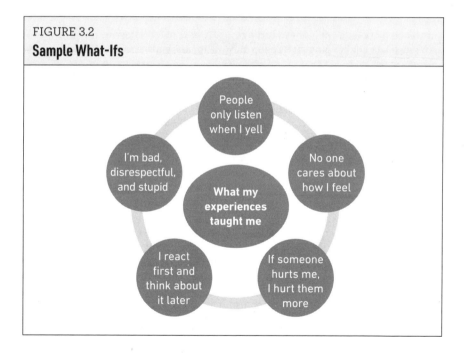

Mindful Reflection for Greater Cultural Humility

Begin by setting your intention. Take a deep breath and remember that mindfulness asks you to allow yourself to nonjudgmentally accept your thoughts and feelings for what they are. They are not good or bad; they simply reflect your authentic reality.

Next, take a couple deep breaths and consider the extent to which you believe that your students and their families are no different from you in their humanity—meaning they would behave just like you and the people in your circle if they had your life experiences, resources, challenges, and supports. If you believe that their humanity and personhood are no different from yours, then you must look to their life experiences to understand their perspective, thoughts, and behaviors.

Continue taking deep breaths as you reflect on a student who exhibits behaviors that you struggle to understand. Then follow these steps:

1. Get a blank sheet of paper and write a description of one recurring emotional or behavioral pattern that you find difficult to understand.
2. List some reasons why a student might exhibit this emotional or behavioral pattern.
3. Think about everything you know about the student's life outside school and write down at least two what-ifs that might explain how the student learned the emotional or behavioral pattern.
4. Identify three questions that you can ask this student or their caregivers to check your assumptions and learn more about who they are, what they have experienced, and what supports they need to be successful at school.
5. After you have checked your assumptions and learned more, write down at least one thing that you can do differently to balance your classroom management expectations with the need to meet this student where they are.

Understanding the perspectives of those who have background and life experiences that are significantly different from our own is intentional work that can be especially challenging for educators who live most of their lives in the dominant cultural position. Get into the habit of continuously challenging your core beliefs about the students who present the most challenges. What are your beliefs about those students? Do you believe that they want to experience success at school, or do you think they are coming to school for the purpose of causing disruptions? Hint: Almost all human beings desperately desire acceptance, belonging, and mastery (McLeod, 2007).

Develop Your Practice

Ideally, teaching mindfulness to your students begins with developing your own personal practice. As you practice mindfulness for your personal well-being, you will develop mindful ways of being that you can bring to all interactions with your students and colleagues.

The more you embody mindfulness, the greater your awareness of how your emotions and actions affect others. The more present you are in your interactions with students, the more you will notice the subtleties of students' verbal and nonverbal expressions. This is a critical aspect of understanding and developing deeper connections with students, especially those who come from different cultural and socioeconomic backgrounds.

You can integrate mindfulness into your daily routine by incorporating it alongside daily habits. Taking advantage of the abundance of guided practices available online is one of the simplest and most accessible ways to develop your personal mindfulness practice. A simple online search will return numerous free guided resources from trained practitioners.

Following are some mindfulness practices that you can integrate into your school day.

Breath Mantra

Integrate this breath mantra into your routine of walking through the school doors, down the hallway, and into your classroom or office:

- Slowly say "breathe in, breathe out" to yourself as you walk, either silently or out loud.
- As you say the mantra, take a deep inhale followed by a deep exhale.
- Notice what is happening around you as you walk—notice your shoes, the floor, the walls, and any people that you pass.
- Without judgment, notice the emotions that you feel as you walk through the door, down the hallway, and into your classroom or office.
- Without judgment, notice the emotions you feel in response to the people you see along the way.

Breath Signals

Integrate breath signals into different parts of your day, such as when the change bell rings, when an announcement is made over the intercom, or when someone knocks at your door:

- When the time arrives, take at least one deep, extended belly breath.
- Each deep breath you take sends a message to your brain to slow down and relax. The brain then sends this message to your body.
- Imagine the breath traveling through your body, passing through points of tension, and exiting out into the present moment.
- Once this practice becomes routine, add this additional step: with each deep breath, and without judgment, scan your physical, mental, and emotional states.

Standing Meditation

Integrate a standing meditation into the start of any transition, such as when transitioning to lunch, prep period, or a parent meeting. This can also be done as a sitting meditation based on your mobility needs:

- Place your arms by your sides and your feet shoulder-width distance apart.
- Focus on the soles of your feet. Feel the connection between your feet and the ground.
- Adjust your feet and your posture so that you feel strong and grounded from the tips of your toes to the top of your head.
- Move your shoulders back so that you are in an upright position, with your chest slightly lifted. This allows you to get the most of each breath.
- Take a full, deep breath and then release it. Again, notice the connection between your feet and the ground, and scan the rest of your body for tension.
- Press your feet to the ground again, move your shoulders back so that you're in an upright position, take another deep breath in, and as you release it, relax any areas of tension. Allow yourself to release the stress and soften your body. Repeat this final step three times.

Mindful End-of-Day Routine

Create a mindful end-of-day routine to intentionally pause the stressors of the day so you can be present for the other aspects of your life that need attention. Can you build a transition routine into your way home from work? If you walk, it can be as simple as intentionally adding a loop around a block by taking a left instead of a right and doing some focused deep breathing to clear your mind before opening your front door. If you drive, consider listening to a podcast or audio book so that your time in traffic adds to your day instead of detracting from it.

The Three-Minute Breathing Space

Mindfulness asks you to attend to your thoughts, your breath, and your body. You can do this in short, three-minute increments of intentional mindfulness:

- In the first minute, simply notice the thoughts that come to mind without feeling the need to change or judge them; just notice and let go.
- During the second minute, narrow your attention to just your breath as you breathe in and out.
- During the third minute, widen your attention to your whole body and, without judgment, notice any sensations that you feel.

Check out the following guided audios for the Three-Minute Breathing Space practice and find one that works for you:

- "The Breathing Space by Jon Kabat Zinn"
  —www.youtube.com/watch?v=8oWmGJc8NWI
- "Mindfulness Meditation 3 Minute Breathing Space"
  —www.youtube.com/watch?v=rOne1POTKL8
- "3-Minute Mindful Breathing Meditation"
  —https://www.youtube.com/watch?v=wPoj5log_7M

Mindfulness-Integrated Pedagogy

Mindfulness through focused breath awareness is a useful tool for transitioning through classroom exercises, resetting when feelings of frustration arise, and returning to the present moment when you catch your thoughts drifting. Take a seven-second breath to center yourself in the present moment:

- Slowly breathe in while counting out three seconds.
- Slowly breathe out while counting out four seconds.
- As you breathe, keep your eyes open or closed based on what works best for you.

Mindfully Managing Emotions in the Classroom

By mindfully reflecting on challenging interactions with students, you can strengthen your ability to model mindful coping and responsive practices rather than reactive decision making in response to stress (Jennings, 2015):

- Reflect on a student you find challenging in some way.
- Think of the last time interactions with this student made it hard for you to teach class.
- Without judgment, identify and name the emotions that you are feeling.
- Notice how your body is reacting to the memory (e.g., tensed shoulders, knotted stomach).
- Don't attempt to halt the feelings or change your perspective on them; just sit with them without judgment and pay attention to any thoughts that emerge.
- Breathe slowly and deeply until any distressing emotions subside.

Repeatedly practicing mindfulness will build your capacity to approach all of life's experiences with less judgment, whether directed at yourself or at others. This enables you to become more curious and welcoming of the full range of life experiences—good and bad—and less afraid of uncomfortable information and feedback. One of the reasons mindful educators are equipped to see their students' side of difficult interactions is that they utilize multiple perspectives when responding to dysregulated behaviors (Skinner & Beers, 2016).

The repeated practice of mindfulness downregulates physiological and mental stress reactivity and upregulates physiological and mental relaxation responses. Specifically, mindfulness affects the following:

- **Reactions to and appraisals of stressful events.** Mindfulness dissuades you from evaluating events as either "good" or "bad," while promoting curiosity and openness in interactions (even when the outcome is uncertain).
- **Instinctive responses in the face of threats.** Mindfulness reduces impulsivity and emotional volatility while making you aware that the urge to react impulsively is temporary.
- **Regulation of strong instinctive responses.** Mindfulness reduces any tendency to either follow or suppress impulses and promotes waiting for input from cognitive, emotional, and sensory systems to register before acting.
- **Coping interactions during stressful episodes.** Mindfulness ensures that you fully engage with stressful events and those involved in them.
- **How you assess stressful episodes afterward.** Mindfulness encourages you to reflect on stressful events and to cultivate a compassionate understanding of students' off-task and dysregulated behaviors.
- **Learning and growth after stressful events.** Mindfulness makes it less likely that you will place the blame for stressful events either on yourself or on others and more likely that you will feel gratitude for such events, recognizing that they often provide opportunities to learn and grow.

Finding PEACE

Consider the table in Figure 3.3., based on the work of Ernest Solar (2013). The more you work to find PEACE within yourself, the more likely that you'll find peace in your interactions with students.

FIGURE 3.3
Finding PEACE

	Action	Definition	Description
P	**Pause**	*Pause* when you become aware of a difficult situation.	Stop everything you are doing, close your eyes, and take a big deep breath.
E	**Exhale**	*Exhale* a sigh, groan, or moan. Then inhale and continue to breathe.	Exhale each breath with an audible sound. Then breathe again.
A	**Acknowledge, Accept, and Allow**	*Acknowledge* and recognize the situation as it is, whether you like it or not. *Accept* the situation and your reaction to it without judgment. *Allow* the experience to happen.	Observe your situation and your reaction from a bird's-eye view without judgment. Simply let it happen without getting mad at yourself for your actions or feelings.
C	**Choose Clarity**	*Choose* how you will respond to the situation and your emotions while maintaining *clarity* about what you want.	It's okay to take minutes, days, or weeks to choose your response to a situation or to your emotions. You may have to respond sooner than you'd like, but always clarify your limits and be compassionate—and don't forget to laugh.
E	**Engage**	*Engage* with people, with the situation, and with life again.	If you feel you cannot do this alone, find someone you trust to help you.

Source: Adapted from "An Alternative Approach to Behavior Interventions: Mindfulness-Based Stress Reduction," by E. Solar, 2013, *Beyond Behavior 22*(2). Copyright 2013 by SAGE Publishing.

4

Mindfulness to Strengthen Student Self-Regulation

When trauma remains unaddressed and unacknowledged, it can become a lens through which children process all subsequent experiences, thus preventing them from fully engaging in the present moment. Thankfully, mindfulness is a practice that you can develop along with your students (Albrecht, Albrecht, & Cohen, 2012). Practicing mindfulness on your own strengthens your ability to demonstrate it to your students. Throughout your career, you will have many opportunities to model mindful self-management during challenging interactions with students, their families, and colleagues.

Whole-class mindfulness practices are an excellent tool to help you manage the wide range of student self-regulation capacities. By engaging the whole class in mindfulness, you are shaping and reshaping your students' brains in ways that improve their cognitive control over emotional reactivity (Modinos, Ormel, & Aleman, 2010; Roeser & Peck, 2009).

Regularly engaging students in mindfulness practices will build their capacity to demonstrate the following executive functioning skills associated with school success (Lyins & DeLange, 2016):

- Selectively focus attention.
- Sustain focused attention.
- Flexibly respond to changing demands.

- Inhibit inappropriate responses.
- Moderate emotional reactivity to stress.

A trauma responsive approach to mindfulness in schools is based on strong educator–student relationships. As a trauma responsive educator, you must be aware of instances when engaging in mindfulness is not helping individual students. Depending on what students have experienced or are currently experiencing, several common mindfulness practices, such as closing one's eyes and taking deep breaths, sitting still in one's seat, or remaining silent, can be triggers for anxiety.

Asking all students to close their eyes may work well for you or even for most students in class, but it may be harmful for students whose traumatic experiences are triggered by flashbacks when they do this. Similarly, sitting in one position for a long time would be counterproductive for students who feel most relaxed when kneeling rather than sitting in their chair.

The goal of mindfulness in schools is to help students improve their thinking and self-regulation by creating a mental gap or headspace between experiencing an emotion from a situation and responding to that situation—not to turn students into meditation masters.

Mindfulness Core Practice

Mindfulness utilizes a limited number of core practices that can be repeated in an endless variety of ways. Alone or in combination, these practices develop students' ability to maintain present-moment awareness both of their experiences and of their physiological and emotional reactions to experiences:

Breathing Practices

- Breathing deeply to send oxygen throughout your body and relaxation signals to your brain.
- Focusing on your breath to maintain present-moment awareness and to gently return awareness to the present when your attention has wandered.

- Focusing on your breath to moderate emotional reactivity to challenges.

Focused Attention Practices

- Sustaining moment-to-moment attention on a specific item or experience (the waning sound of a chime, a single thought or word, your own breathing).
- Noticing (without judgment) when your attention strays and gently returning your focus to the focal item or experience.
- Selectively clearing and focusing a distracted mind.

Body Scanning Practices

- Intentionally and nonjudgmentally attending to all aspects of your physical state in the present moment.
- Attending to your body to maintain present-moment awareness and, when necessary, to gently refocus your attention to specific aspects of your physical state.
- Recognizing the stress and emotional reactivity that you hold and express through your physical well-being.

Open Monitoring Practices

- Expanding your present-moment attention to take in the totality of what is happening.
- Being nonjudgmentally aware of any experience that enters your consciousness.
- Sitting with all your mental and emotional states as well as all present external stimuli without feeling the need to immediately push away the experience.

As students repeatedly practice letting go of objects and distractions and returning their focus to the present moment, they strengthen their ability to focus on a goal without getting distracted. This effortful regulation will have cascading benefits for meeting behavioral and academic expectations in educational contexts (Lyins & DeLange, 2016).

How Mindfulness Restores Agency in Those Coping with Trauma

Very often, the minds of students faced with trauma can be consumed with intrusive thoughts that distract them from their present-moment experience in the classroom. The anxiety this creates can trigger emotional and behavioral dysregulation.

Chronically stressed children can appear as hyperaroused—students who are highly active and reactive, and overly sensitive to stimulation—or hypoaroused—students who struggle to become engaged, have little energy, and are slow to process your statements. Yet others fluctuate quickly between these two states: overreactive one moment and then struggling to stay awake several moments later.

Each time distressing emotions are triggered, cortisol, adrenaline, and other stress hormones flood the brain and body. This overproduction of hormones and neurochemicals hinders the ongoing development of higher order brain structures like the hippocampus (which affects our ability to memorize, recall, and learn) and the prefrontal cortex (which affects information processing and rational decision making) (Compas, 2006). Thankfully, children's brains can and do change in response to new experiences. This means that educators can provide developmentally supportive experiences that, with repeated practice, will help children cultivate less emotionally reactive, more mindful coping responses (Schore, 2003).

Mindfulness practices are beneficial for all children but may be especially helpful for children coping with traumatic life experiences that induce dysregulation. For many of these children, school may be the one place where they regularly experience what calm feels like, and educators may be the primary adults who take time to teach them the self-regulation skills needed to succeed in life.

Effortful Emotional Regulation

The emphasis that mindfulness places on strengthening emotional regulation is particularly beneficial for students coping with trauma (Gross, 1998). By learning to sit with unpleasant emotions and notice that they are temporary, we learn not to escape or suppress any given emotional experience (Galla et al., 2016). When we allow negative emotions to simply *be* without actively attempting to push them away, they become less salient. Paradoxically, attempting to push away negative emotions only makes them more salient (Wegner, 1994).

By improving emotion regulation, mindfulness makes us less vulnerable to negative emotional events by slowing the activation of our stress systems (Blair & Diamond, 2008; Davidson et al., 2003). In fact, those who practice mindfulness have more activation in the brain areas that moderate emotional responses to threat than those who don't (Brown, Weinstein, & Creswell, 2012).

For traumatized students, school success may require learning to "inhibit the activation of a strong but maladaptive response, [and increasing] the activation of a weak but adaptive response" (Galla et al., 2016). Consider, for example, a student who strikes out when someone bumps them in a crowded hallway. This student will need to learn to inhibit this strong maladaptive reaction by adding a gap between initial perception and reaction so that they have enough time to allow for present-moment awareness of themselves, others, and the situational context. This kind of effortful regulation—that is, replacing an intense desire to react with a considered response—can be strengthened through regular mindfulness practice.

Differentiation and Mindfulness

Mindfulness works with students from all racial, ethnic, and socioeconomic backgrounds. Though it may be introduced in different ways and the specific terms used may vary, the core practices and intentions remain the same. One study found that a 12-week, 45-minute daily mindfulness training was associated with significant reductions in maladaptive reactions to stress among urban, low-income 4th and 5th grade students (Mendelson et al., 2010).

Not all students will immediately want to engage in mindfulness. It is important to consider whether students feel safe before expecting them to do so. It is also important to invite students to engage at whatever level feels comfortable to them. For example, a student may want to keep their eyes open or just sit quietly and listen to the audio. You can be trauma responsive during whole-class mindfulness practices by continually scanning for increased agitation in students (whether it's expressed verbally or nonverbally). Following are some indicators that you need to take a student aside and privately ask them how they are experiencing mindfulness:

- Difficulty taking the activity seriously.
- Being triggered by silence because it lets in uncomfortable memories and emotions.
- Displaying avoidance behaviors.
- Being unable to stop talking, laughing, or fidgeting.
- Verbally expressing a distaste for mindfulness activities.

Emotional distress due to poor coping skills is the underlying cause of many behavior challenges. Helping students develop the ability to mindfully experience and process distressing events will enable them to engage in more self-reflective and self-regulated decision making before responding to those events (Broderick & Metz, 2016).

As you contemplate how you can use mindfulness to strengthen students' social and emotional skills, remember that it is never to be used as a reactive consequence for off-task and dysregulated behaviors. It is to be proactively taught and responsibly used to help students self-regulate. The difference between the two is all in how you invite students into the practice. *Don't* say, in a firm and demanding tone, "Because you are too talkative, I am going to stop the class to do mindfulness." *Do* say, in a firm but inviting tone, "It seems like we have lost focus on the task at hand, so let's all pause our work and take a moment to use the Three-Minute Breathing Space practice to calm our bodies and refocus our thoughts."

You must meet students where they are when you begin practicing mindfulness, allowing space for those who initially resist by requiring the minimum from them, which is that they sit quietly and not disrupt others.

You can help them to meet this expectation by giving them the option to quietly complete another activity, such as coloring a mindful maze.

Use the following strategies when working with students for whom the feeling of calm or inner awareness is new or unsettling:

- Invite them to participate with the class and make explicitly clear that they can also quietly observe without participating as the class engages with mindfulness.
- Invite them to participate with the class and provide an alternative silent activity should they decline to participate.
- Provide additional reminders that they can keep their eyes open if they feel any discomfort; offer a focus object such as a stone or small statue for those who wish to keep their eyes open.
- Include whole-class mindfulness practices that are better suited for traumatized children, such as mindful mazes and movement-based mindfulness practices.
- Acknowledge and celebrate any attempt at mindfulness, no matter how small.
- Share your own experiences with your developing mindfulness practice.

You must allow your students to express their individual differences when engaging with mindfulness and account for variations in the time it takes them to buy into it. The core practices of breathing, focused attention, body scanning, and open monitoring are applicable to all age groups and are made developmentally appropriate by attending to the cognitive, emotional, and physical needs of each individual. When necessary, consider the following developmentally appropriate modifications suggested by Lyins and DeLange (2016):

- Keeping exercises short (two to five minutes).
- Using aids like coloring sheets and puzzles.
- Having students stand or move around during exercises.
- Employing resources that use words, images, and animation to engage students.

Introducing Mindfulness to Students

As you introduce mindfulness to students, remember to continue developing your self-compassion. Being gentle toward yourself will allow you to do the same for your students. Focusing your students' present-moment attentions with mindfulness should allow for fewer worries and less rumination, leaving more space for learning. However, developing mindfulness among your students, like any other skill, takes time, practice, and room to make errors. Your own personal experiences practicing mindfulness will strengthen your ability to integrate it into your teaching.

Here are some important considerations to keep in mind as you prepare to introduce mindfulness to your students:

Introduce mindfulness with less talking and more action. Mindfulness can appear abstract when introduced with words; talking is rarely used as a means of practicing mindfulness. It is important that students of all ages begin to explore mindfulness through guided actions. Rather than explain mindful breathing, demonstrate for your students and have them repeat.

Never force students. The benefits of mindfulness are not meant to be forced upon anyone; this is particularly important for students. If a student is not open to mindfulness, then the benefits will never be realized. Use your pedagogical knowledge and personal experiences practicing mindfulness to gauge why a student may be hesitant to practice and respond with kindness and respect. Invite non-participating students to do a quiet activity in order to respect the other students in their practice while remaining in the room.

Keep a light-hearted perspective. As an individual practitioner of mindfulness, you may know firsthand how difficult it is to start and maintain a mindfulness practice. Keeping your expectations reasonable and remembering that mindfulness is not about achievement can reengage your commitment to mindfulness and your classroom when the tougher days come through, and they will come. Remember to honor yourself and your students' efforts for the small wins.

Not every day is going to be amazing. Adding mindfulness concepts to your classroom routine means it is important to account for days where even a one-minute mindfulness practice seems like a struggle. On these days, simply pausing to engage all students in a slow three-breath mindful moment at some point during the class is a good way to be consistent. Be kind to your students and yourself by feeling happy with any amount of progress.

Use brevity to keep students' attentions. It is common for educators to feel as though they can barely keep students' attentions with the typical teaching routine. Fortunately, mindfulness can be kept brief or intertwined with pre-existing class routines such as a two-minute mindful practice to center all students before beginning to line up to go to the lunchroom. Add longer intervals of mindfulness when possible, but do not be afraid to vary the mindfulness practice with creativity and different exercises. Take pride in consistency rather than perfection.

Build students' mindful vocabulary. Building student vocabulary bridges the practices done in the classroom with their lives outside school and increases the likelihood that they will generalize it as more than just something done in the classroom. It is also important for educators throughout the school to use a common language for mindfulness. This ensures that students receive consistent messages as they move from one educator to another, from one space like the library to another like the specials class, and from one grade to the next. Call-to-action phrases such as "checking in" or "listen to your inner voice" can help clarify key aspects of mindfulness that work in and out of the classroom.

Attending to Equity by Practicing Culturally Responsive Mindfulness

Culturally responsive teaching means adjusting your curriculum, instructional practices, and ways of interacting with students based on knowledge and awareness of the students in your school and classroom. Another way of saying this is that the content and delivery of instruction has been prepared with this specific group of students in mind. It is important to ensure that your approach to mindfulness is culturally responsive as well. Western mindfulness has been steeped in a culture of secular Whiteness and often uses the language of individualism, which can limit the extent to which educators and students from diverse backgrounds view it as relevant to their lives (Williams & Kabat-Zinn, 2013).

Introducing mindfulness in ways that center students of color should not be new or controversial; contemplative practices have long existed in every country and culture on earth. Educators must understand that there is no culturally neutral way of implementing mindfulness practices and should thus adapt practices through thoughtful consideration of the ways of being that students bring with them into the classroom.

The overwhelming majority of mindfulness videos developed for children and schools are presented by a White woman delivering the lesson in a "measured, whispered, monotonic voice, [which] can be experienced as unfamiliar, 'weird,' or inconsistent with cultural values of authentic expressiveness, and can be perceived as overcontrolled, detached, and impersonal" (Harrell, 2018, p. 28). Educators using videos and audios to introduce mindfulness to students of color should consider whether students are able to see themselves and their culture reflected in the teaching tools used.

Here are some possible cultural adaptations you might make for students from underrepresented backgrounds:

- Use a broad range of culturally diverse calming music, such as lo-fi hip-hop, jazz, bossa nova, indigenous American spiritual chanting, or other culturally centered music.
- Find resources that feature presenters from a range of racial and ethnic groups.
- Include non-White individuals and animated characters when demonstrating practices.

Consider introducing mindfulness through video clips of athletes and artists from your students' culture talking about their own mindfulness practices. Consider using passages from poetry, socially conscious music, or images from graphic artists that communicate the principles of mindfulness.

Cultural responsiveness is not about reinventing the wheel. Your job as a culturally responsive educator is to communicate and practice mindfulness "in ways that are in synch with the rhythms of how [your students] experience and understand their own lives" (Harrell, 2018, p. 31).

I encourage educators who have done the work of developing their own critical understanding of race and racialization to use mindfulness to help their students critically process their race-related thoughts, feelings, and experiences. Search for and utilize guided practices such as the Black Lives Matter Meditation for Healing Racial Trauma meditation (Nicole, 2016).

Using Mindfulness as an Educational Tool

There are at least three ways you can use mindfulness as an educational tool in your classroom:

1. **As a daily practice.** Use mindfulness at predictable times of each day when students need help bringing down their levels of arousal and focusing their thoughts on learning, such as when they first arrive at school and after lunch and recess. Daily practice is the most effective way for students to build mindfulness skills.

2. **As a planned brief mindfulness break.** Use mindfulness strategically as an attentional aid during extended academic activities. These short *brain breaks* prevent cognitive exhaustion.

3. **As a supportive response to unpredicted stressors.** When things happen that make students feel anxious, fearful, angry, or distressed, remind them to practice the mindfulness skills they have learned to attain a state of calm.

Following are some examples of mindfulness exercises you can integrate into daily practice.

A Mindful Transition to the Start of Class

Requires: A computer or smartphone, speakers, and a "please wait, we are practicing mindfulness" sign

When to implement: At the start of class

Steps:

- Before students enter the classroom, open a mindfulness resource on a computer or smartphone synced to a speaker.
- As students enter, remind them that class will begin with mindfulness.
- As soon as class begins, place the "please wait, we are practicing mindfulness" sign on the door.
- Ask anyone who arrives late to wait just outside the door for the duration of the mindfulness practice.
- Turn lights down or off and place a focusing object like a large rock atop a desk. Remind students that they may close their eyes or direct their attention to the focusing object.
- State that mindfulness will now begin and press play on the computer or phone.
- Students and educator both practice mindfulness to begin the class.

Spiral Maze

Requires: A printed spiral maze

When to implement: In the middle of an extended lecture or individual seated assignment

Steps:

- During a lesson that requires extended instruction or digesting a lot of material, make space and time for a 5-minute mindfulness refocusing break.
- If students are engrossed in the learning task, make sure to give them 2-minute and 1-minute reminders that a 5-minute mindfulness break will soon begin.

- When ready, state that the mindfulness break is about to begin and pass out a printed spiral maze. (You can find mazes online at websites such as at relax4life.com and mazestoprint.com.)
- By shifting to this activity, students can reset their minds and reinvigorate their concentration.
- Make sure to alternate between a variety of mazes.

Whole-Class Mindfulness Chime

Requires: A computer or smartphone and speakers to play a simulated chime

When to implement: When several students are exhibiting off-task behaviors, distracted attention, or excessive talking

Steps:
- During times when students are calm, introduce them to the mindfulness chime.
- Instruct them to focus on the sound of the chime and to silently take deep breaths in and out until the ringing completely ceases.
- This silent breath practice is particularly useful during the early stages of increasing agitation and distraction.
- Here are just a few of the mindfulness chime resources designed for students that are available online:
  — "Introducing Children to Chime Meditation" by Diane R. Gehart (www.youtube.com/watch?v=LPe6aP06kZQ)
  — "Mindful Minute" by GoZen (www.youtube.com/watch?v=ZME0JKiweL4)
  — "Mindfulness Bell" by The Guided Meditation Site (www.youtube.com/watch?v=wGFog-OuFDM)

One note of caution: overuse of these kinds of attention-getters can undermine their effectiveness as students become desensitized to them.

Individual Student Mindfulness Space

Requires: A designated space in the classroom stocked with calming props and decorations

When to implement: When an individual appears distracted, on edge, frustrated, or anxious

Steps:

- Prepare a specific area in the classroom to invite feelings of calm.
- Whenever you think a student may need a moment to reset, invite them to spend a few minutes in the mindfulness space.
- Students should also feel welcome to move into the mindfulness space when they themselves feel they need a short break from the classroom or lesson.
- Although educators may consider limiting the amount of time students have in the mindfulness space, they should also teach and encourage students to self-manage their use of the space.

Informal Mindfulness Practices

There are many ways to integrate mindful ways of being throughout the school day (Sheinman et al., 2018; Tornio, 2018). For example, something as simple as shifting how students answer questions in class lets them experience the benefits of slowing down and reflecting before responding. By adding a wait time, they can think more deeply and critically before answering questions. Teach them the term *wait time* and instructions; let students know you will "pause for three seconds after asking the class a question before selecting a student to answer. After an answer is provided, I will wait three seconds for whole-class reflection before I respond to the answer." Those three seconds have been found to improve students' higher-order thinking skills (Honea, 1982). Make sure to let your students know that wait time is a mindfulness practice.

Here are some additional informal mindfulness practices to consider:

- Remind students to breathe deeply before, during, and after exams; this stimulates the bodily systems responsible for calming you down.
- Use visual aids and other tactile materials in the classroom to remind students about and prompt them to engage in mindfulness.
- Introduce a new mindfulness word or phrase each week and have students interact with it in different ways (e.g., by drawing them out

or using sentence frames). A few starter examples include *present moment, body scan, use your breath, checking-in, centering,* and *be in the here and now.*

- Use terms such as "checking in" and "nonjudgmental" to clarify key aspects of mindfulness.
- Create mindfulness interactions through games, coloring sheets, or in-class stretches.
- Read from a book that introduces mindfulness, such as *The Lemonade Hurricane* (2015) by Licia Morelli.

Addressing Challenges

As you practice mindfulness along with your students, you will likely experience a few common hurdles. As you learn to overcome these, you will be able to help your students do the same.

Self-Criticism

Judging ourselves while practicing mindfulness is very common. The purpose of mindfulness is not to empty your thoughts or remove all negativity; it is to be fully present in the moment. If you think self-critical thoughts, acknowledge them, try letting them go, and remind yourself that mindfulness is not about achievement.

Sleepiness

If you are practicing mindfulness in a state of bodily exhaustion, you may find yourself drifting to sleep rather than practicing mindfulness. Practice with your eyes open and focus on an object or opt for a walking or standing practice. Adapt your personal practice of mindfulness to your body's needs in the moment.

Restlessness

A racing mind can make it hard to settle into the practice of mindfulness. If the busyness of life is intruding on your thoughts while you practice, consider using a focusing object to calm your mind. Another option is square breathing, where you trace your fingers along the edges of a page and breathe in and out while running your finger along each edge.

Checking in with Students

Regularly check-in with yourself and your students to determine if you need to adjust the use of mindfulness in your classroom. Consider these planning questions to increase success:

- What times during the day are most stressful for me and for students?
- When do my students struggle to focus? During what times of the day and what activities?
- Do some students need additional guidance to learn how to engage in mindfulness?

To reinforce students' use of mindfulness for academic success, infuse mindful inquiry into your teaching. For example, you might ask students to slowly trace their fingers over each letter in the title of the textbook while taking slow, deep breaths to prepare themselves to focus on math class. Or provide students with a one- to three-minute "pause-and-reflect time" after you describe an in-class assignment but before they begin working. The goal is to have students quietly reflect on their thinking before beginning individual or group work. They can jot notes or doodle on a blank sheet while thinking about the assignment.

Mindful Alternatives to Detention

You can use mindfulness to transform how you respond to students when they make behavioral errors. A few pioneering schools, such as Robert W. Coleman Elementary School and Patterson Park High School in Baltimore, have shifted away from using a traditional detention room where students stare helplessly at the wall, out the window, or at the room monitor. Traditional detention does nothing to help students reflect on and learn from whatever got them sent to detention, so they return to the classroom having lost instructional time and without any improvements in their social and emotional skills.

Administrators at both schools realized that their students, many of whom were growing up in adverse contexts, were being punished for having compromised self-regulation and executive functioning skills due to trauma. With support from the Holistic Life Foundation, they shifted to mindful detention by creating a "Mindful Moment Room"—a physically comfortable and comforting space where educators guided students through mindfulness practices to help them calm, reflect, and recenter before returning to the classroom or other activities. The shift to mindful detention was supported by other opportunities to practice mindfulness throughout the school day. Both schools reported dramatic reductions in behavior challenges and suspensions and increased attendance after implementing these changes.

The goal of a mindful alternative to detention is to ensure that schools don't retraumatize children by punishing them for the very predictable dysregulation caused by trauma. A mindful detention room should be comfortable and calming for students, allowing them to deescalate, reflect on their behavior, and add to or strengthen their coping skills before returning to class. The environment should be made warm and calming through lighting, color, pictures, and comfortable seating.

Students should be in the mindful detention room for no longer than 30 minutes to minimize loss of instructional time. However, there will be times when a longer stay will be beneficial to ensure that students have fully deescalated. All room facilitators must have training in deescalation and supportive behavior management.

Stations should be set up at desks or on floor rugs in the room to enable students to move through the following sequence of activities. Have several beanbags or rug squares for students to sit on when they enter the room so their bodies can calm before moving to the desks. To minimize unproductive discussions when students are escalated, visuals with each step of the process outlined here should be posted around the room that you can point to, when needed, to guide students:

1. **Greet.** Each student should be greeted warmly by the adult facilitating the room. When students are in an escalated state, focus on

ensuring they feel safe. Conversations with students about their behavior can happen after they feel both calm and safe.

2. **Tune in.** The first thing all students should be taught to do is to listen and feel their own heart beating. Teach them to come in, get comfortable, and look down or close their eyes, place a hand over their heart, and listen to and feel their heartbeat. Prompt them to notice if their heart is beating fast or thumping hard and to listen quietly until it begins to slow down. They can do this before starting the mindfulness session or as they wait for their turn to use the mindfulness headphones (see next step).

3. **Cool down.** Students should now use a set of mindfulness headphones attached to inexpensive music players loaded with a limited number of mindfulness audios they can select. The aim is to engage students in a reflective and calming mindfulness practice to shift their brain into learning mode. If all headphones are being used, students should be directed to wait on the rug or one of the beanbags. The amount of time that students will need to calm down varies based on the students' self-regulation skills, how escalated they were at the start, and other individual factors.

4. **Reflect.** Provide students with a brief reflection worksheet that will help them think through their problem and brainstorm solutions. Students should take an open seat and complete the reflection worksheet with words or pictures, as appropriate. They can ask the room facilitator for help as needed.

5. **Talk it out.** Once students complete the reflection sheet, they discuss it with the room facilitator. The role of the room facilitator is to actively listen to students' perspectives, understand the student's actions and their perception of the actions of others, and explore any underlying causes of their behavior. This discussion will often include helping the student learn how to name and manage their emotions, learn how to express their emotions in appropriate ways, see how their actions affect others, and understand the perspectives of other persons involved.

6. **Get back to class or classwork.** If the student is calm and has been able to think through some next steps or has control of their emotions, they should return to class. If "talking it out" has caused the student's emotions to escalate or the student is otherwise not ready to return to class, the student should not return. Instead, they should remain in the room to engage in individual work from a prepared grade-level work packet, read a book, or work on assignments sent by their classroom teacher.

7. **Take brain breaks.** For students who must remain in the room doing academic work beyond the 30-minute recommended time limit, the room facilitator should collectively engage all students in a brief active brain break every half-hour.

Shifting to a mindful alternative to detention needs to be supported with other interventions throughout the school that strengthen students' social and emotional skills. For example, after working with one school to initiate this process, we quickly realized that students in one classroom were "getting into trouble" just so they could be sent to detention. After debriefing with students, it became clear that for many of them, the classroom was unsafe and triggering. The remedy was to help the teacher understand how students were experiencing some of her behavior management practices. This resulted in a gradual transformation of the culture and climate of her classroom.

5

Understanding Students' Needs for Safety at School

For students coping with traumatic stressors, schools and classrooms are spaces not only for learning but also for experiencing the moments of safety and calm necessary to learn how to trust in themselves and others. As educational journalist Sara Bernard (2010) has stated, creating a safe learning environment "may not be rocket science, but it sure is neuro-science" (para. 1). It is indeed important to keep the neuroscience of trauma responsive educational practices in mind.

Punitive consequences for dysregulated behaviors are in opposition to the ways that our brains respond to threats. When people feel threatened, their decision-making functions are under the control of their emotional and instinctive brains rather than their thinking brains. Their ability to form neural connections that encode and retrieve learning is therefore undermined. This means that students who view you as a threatening disciplinarian will struggle to learn. Their focus is on processing the concrete and immediately actionable aspects of the situation rather than on abstract learning.

What's more, children coping with trauma—those whose brains and bodies are constantly activated by stress—develop a heightened level of negative reactivity to potentially threatening events. This means that they will be more easily agitated and have difficulty regaining calm if they feel threatened. For such students to learn, they need to trust that they are in a safe space where they can reduce their hypervigilance to threat and shift their attention to learning academic content. This need for safety has long been established as a foundational need that must be attended to before more abstract aspects of self and interpersonal development can flourish (Maslow, 1943).

The need to experience school as a safe space is especially critical for students in high-crime neighborhoods who navigate real threats on a regular basis. These students have learned that they need to be hypervigilant to stay safe because they cannot expect that others have created a safe environment for them.

Warm Demanders

Investing time creating physical, psychological, and emotional safety does not detract from, but rather facilitates, rigorous instruction. Educators who attend to students' needs for safety while continuing to hold students to high expectations are often referred to as "warm demanders" (Bondy et al., 2007). In contrast to "uncompromising disciplinarians," warm demanders balance high expectations with high support. Students in classrooms led by warm demanders are both cared for and held accountable for upholding behavioral standards. Warm demanders establish a culture of high expectations and mutual respect—for the educator, for peers, and for the learning environment.

The term *warm demander* was originally used to describe an educator of Athabaskan Indian and Eskimo students (Kleinfeld, 1975). The warm demander engages in a culturally situated practice by recognizing that students of color, particularly those who are also coping with adversity and interpersonal trauma, will respect and follow educators who establish *earned* authority over those who attempt to enforce institutional authority. Many students of color or their family members and friends have been harmed by abuses of institutional authority—"Do as I say because the system has given me power and authority over you." Therefore, they need a safe learning environment that is created through authority that the educator earns by demonstrating care and respect for student dignity and well-being—"Do as I say because I have shown that I recognize and value your worth."

Insistence is one broadly applicable strategy that warm demanders use. Ross and colleagues (2008) describe insistence as strategies that ensure that students never give up on themselves and that educators never give up on students. Insistence that students meet classroom expectations cannot be for the simple purpose of gaining compliance; rather, it must be for the purpose of creating the conditions that maximize learning among students facing difficult life circumstances. Ross and colleagues emphasize a strategy of "repeat, remind, reinforce, and respond with consequences":

Repeat. The educator responds to students who aren't complying with a behavioral request by firmly, respectfully, and neutrally repeating the request until the student complies. The educator must use a warm tone and refrain from exhibiting frustration or distress.

Remind. The educator prompts students to engage in the expected behavior by reminding them using both verbal and nonverbal communication (such as pointing to a sign or miming the expected behavior). These reminders can come before or after the formally stated behavioral request. There is no punishment associated with the reminders; they are simply another strategy for insisting that students succeed in class.

Reinforce. The educator recognizes and affirms the student when they correct their behavior. This is a critical part of maintaining student motivation. A lot of student misbehavior is motivated by desire for attention, and in many classrooms, students learn that the quickest way to get their educators to see them is to disobey rules. The educator should frequently affirm students for meeting or trying to meet behavioral requests.

Respond with consequences. The educator delivers consequences to students who refuse to follow behavioral requests, but these are directly connected to the behavioral error and help the student learn or practice what to do differently next time. If students are to learn from consequences, the educator cannot deliver them in a tone of frustration or anger and cannot harm student dignity. In addition, the same consequences shouldn't be delivered repeatedly for the same behavioral error. Any behavioral error that occurs repeatedly without improvement should initiate a search for the underlying cause of the problem.

Warm demanders determine the support they give to students based on what they know about students' strengths, learning needs and styles, cultures, and challenges outside school. For example, if a warm demander knows that a particular student has no place to do homework at home, instead of either letting them off the hook or punishing them, the educator will work with them to collaboratively identify alternative ways of meeting the expectation. They may agree that the student will spend time in the library after school, for example, and the educator will help make arrangements with the librarian. The student feels supported by the educator taking the time to listen to the challenges they are facing, respected by the educator for including them in identifying the solution, and affirmed that the educator believes in their ability to succeed. The relationship between the educator and student is strengthened by the positive and neutral, but never punitive, ways that high expectations are clearly and consistently communicated.

A common misperception is that being trauma responsive means lowering expectations for students who are coping with traumatic experiences. In fact, the opposite is true. Several studies report that students in high-poverty, high-crime neighborhoods want schools to be clearly different from the chaos they experience outside school (Wilson & Corbett, 2001). They want educators to create classrooms that are orderly and predictable and that hold clear and consistent high expectations. They want educators who show they believe students are important enough to be taught, respected, and held accountable.

A warm demander creates a safe environment by doing the following:

- Intentionally building relationships with and among students.
- Being self-aware about their own culture and how it differs from students'.
- Clearly and consistently communicating high expectations for both academic achievement and behavior.

- Positively insisting on academic success by making i̇
  sible for students *not* to learn the content.
- Identifying and providing the supports necessary for stu
  meet those high expectations.

Three Categories of Safety

All educators, and especially classroom teachers—the adults with whom students spend most of their day—play key roles in developing and maintaining safety at school. This is not an add-on to educators' already full plates; it happens within the scope of typical pedagogical frameworks and instructional practices. By relying on principles that are trauma responsive, educators can develop classroom environments that are safe, caring, and engaging for all. The default is to focus on physical safety, but it is equally crucial that we attend to psychological and emotional safety. (Each of these aspects of safety is discussed in greater detail and with relevant implementation strategies in separate chapters.)

Physical safety means protection from violence and threats of violence from peers, staff, and any other member of the school community. Physical safety can be threatened by aggressive and profane statements, a kick in the shins, a punch in the shoulder, and fights. Educators must respond to each occurrence, be firm about their nonacceptance, model and teach appropriate ways of interpersonal communication and interaction, and close with restorative justice practices to ensure that feelings of safety are reestablished. Student safety can also be threatened by the physical and sexual actions of adults at school; students need to know that reports of such actions will be believed and investigated.

Psychological safety means protection from derogatory statements and discipline that negatively affect students' sense of self. Maintaining adherence to behavioral expectations should not come at the expense of students' positive sense of themselves as valued members of the school community. The extent to which students feel psychologically safe at school will significantly affect how motivated they are to follow school rules. Disciplinary interactions need to reassure students that they are being held accountable to follow school rules because they are valued members of the school community.

Emotional safety means feeling protected, supported, and enabled to take learning risks, make mistakes, and fail without feeling like a failure. Threats to emotional safety are most likely to occur during instructional time. Students may feel that their input during lessons is not valued or will be met with ridicule. It is essential to establish and reinforce classroom expectations that honor the intellectual contributions of every student and to see mistakes as evidence of learning. When students fear making mistakes, opportunities for growth are compromised.

Behavioral Signs of Feeling Unsafe

Students growing up in unstable environments often find that providing for their own safety is the central issue around which all aspects of their lives are organized. To stay safe, students may need to be hypervigilant on their walk to school. While at school, these same students are preparing for what they may encounter when they leave. And this is all in addition to watching out for peers or educators who may pose a physical, psychological, or emotional threat. These students are easily triggered into heightened states of arousal, and it is exceedingly difficult for them to return to the state of calm that is necessary for learning while at school (Collins, 2001). Following are some ways in which feeling unsafe can manifest in students:

- **Hypervigilance**—watching peers for indications that they may pose a physical, psychological, or emotional threat; tending to interpret interactions as provocative.
- **Preoccupation**—overthinking about undesirable situations or possible threats.
- **Being easily triggered**—getting alarmed by things that most students wouldn't notice; being resistant to calming measures.
- **Irritability**—difficulty modulating sharp, mean, or disrespectful responses to seemingly normal questions and requests.

- **Acting withdrawn**—disconnecting emotionally from people and circumstances as a way to cope with overwhelming, confusing, or triggering feelings.

Many educators do not realize when their students are in a state of hypervigilance and heightened arousal. Trauma responsive classroom management includes strategies to help students meet their needs to

- Receive frequent reassurances that they are safe in school.
- Reduce their learned hypervigilance.
- Achieve a level of internal calm that enables them to focus on learning.

Trauma responsive classroom management is based on understanding the neurobiology of trauma and how it affects behavior, then using that understanding to reframe our view of students' motivations for acting out (Perry, 2006).

Trauma Responsive Mantras

Mantras are statements that can help you stay connected with your intentions and continually make choices that align with them. According to the Chopra Center, a mantra can be thought of as a seed for energizing an intention, and by repeatedly returning to it, it will blossom. Use the following trauma responsive mantras to help ensure you are a safe educator with a safe classroom climate.

"My students want to give me what I want." This mantra is to remind you that students want to be successful in your classroom, so when they fall short of meeting your expectations, you should wonder why rather than become angry. Trauma responsive educators believe that it's the educator's job to identify barriers and provide scaffolds when behavioral expectations are not met.

"My students are doing the best they can with the tools they have." This mantra is to remind you that students' success depends on the skills they have developed and whether those skills match the needs of the context. Try to maintain a growth mindset by persistently believing that behavioral skills can be learned and developed.

"My students are not responsible for their own safety." This mantra is to remind you that creating and maintaining the conditions for optimal learning are your responsibility as an educator. Students must feel safe in their school and especially in their classrooms.

"Engaged classrooms are safe classrooms." This mantra is to remind you that when students' attention is captured by a lesson and there are many opportunities for them to actively engage with the content and experience mastery, all aspects of safety are fostered. In engaged classrooms, educators regularly update lesson plans to connect with students' identities and lives outside school; curate diverse learning resources to enable student choice; and go back and forth between whole-class, small-group, and individual instruction to invite students to own their learning process.

Attending to Equity by Considering Cultural Constructions of Care

Educators are repeatedly told that they need to be able to connect with students in order to teach them. Many educators mistakenly perceive a tension between building relationships with students and holding them accountable for meeting expectations. This can be particularly challenging for White and middle-class educators working in schools serving students from underserved communities exposed to traumatic life experiences. Educators who lack a personal cultural connection to these students run the risk of sympathizing rather than empathizing with students.

Caring is a culturally situated concept that must be interpreted through a critical lens. Otherwise, it can be an "emotion-laden practice characterized by low expectations motivated by taking pity on students' social circumstances . . . and lowering academic expectations of the student out of pity" (Antrop-González & De Jesús, 2006, p. 411). Critical care is emotionally supportive and avoids pity by ensuring that vulnerable students understand they are being held to high standards because you believe in them and will respond with developmentally appropriate supports when they make mistakes.

Student receptivity to critical caring actions is illustrated by some of the examples that Black and Latinx students have shared of what they consider to be caring actions from educators. As Antrop-González and De Jesús (2006) report, students state that educators who care do the following:

- Make themselves available to provide additional academic support.
- Invest time in listening to students' academic and other concerns.
- Ensure that students have understood and mastered the material before moving on.
- Provide opportunities for students to redo assignments and retake tests because they believe that students could do better.
- Are aware of whether students are meeting behavioral expectations and provide guidance and behavioral redirections when students are off task.
- Ask questions that demonstrate their concern about students' safety at school, at home, and in their communities.

Trauma Responsive Language

Trauma responsive educators must ensure that our language, which influences much of what students think about themselves and about what is possible, is itself trauma responsive. Nobel Prize–winning scientist Daniel Kahneman (2005) has estimated that each day we experience approximately 20,000 moments. Our brain keeps track of which moments are positive and which are negative, and the resulting ratio affects our overall well-being. Because negative moments carry much more weight and last in our memories much longer than positive moments, it is important to ensure that most of our language contributes to the latter.

Instinctively focusing on negative moments and retaining them in memory is an evolutionary development that helps us learn from and survive threats (Baumeister et al., 2001). Children coping with trauma tend to look for and hold onto moments that confirm their already negative self-image. We can counter this by ensuring that our language promotes positive self-image, avoids assigning faults to students' character or person, maintains a neutral or positive tone, and expresses empathy and genuine support.

Trauma responsive language prioritizes students' positive self-image and dignity. Dysregulated behavior is a form of communication, and we can listen to that communication to identify lacking or lagging skills and respond in supportive ways. Due to the negative effects of trauma and toxic stress on development, children coping with trauma often struggle to effectively communicate big emotions.

Trauma responsive language rejects punitive, sarcastic, and critical comments that demean student's identities that undermine rather than strengthen your authority. It is important to remember that deescalating situations by remaining emotionally neutral and validating the student's experience is not the same as agreeing with the student. Whenever possible, educators should deliver corrective statements to students in private, as they may embarrass students or be seized upon by other students as an opportunity for bullying. To protect themselves from these outcomes, students may become defiant and aggressive. Unsurprisingly, critical public corrections also damage educator–student relationships by undermining the student's trust in you to keep them safe.

Strengthening Use of Trauma Responsive Language

The ways we communicate with students when they do not meet behavioral and academic expectations will either reinforce a negative self-image or build their sense of themselves as capable of positive growth. By focusing your corrections on skill development that needs to occur, you are holding students accountable without making identity and relationally harmful statements. Using trauma responsive language, especially during emotionally charged interactions, is a skill that will strengthen with practice. The following reflection exercises will help you assess the trauma responsiveness of the language you use in school:

Ask others for feedback. Share your goal of strengthening your use of trauma responsive language with students and colleagues, then invite a few trusted colleagues to let you know when you may need to adjust your language so that students experience it as safe and supportive.

Consider how the behavior is affecting you. Being able to identify your triggers and having present-moment awareness of your emotional state in the middle of a difficult interaction can reduce the likelihood of making harsh and identity harmful statements to students. Ask yourself, "How do I feel about the behavior and how do I feel about the student?" "What is this behavior triggering in me?" "What needs to happen for us to have a positive interaction next time?"

Ask yourself what you can do to improve your relationship with students. Students are much more likely to engage their self-regulation skills when given behavioral corrections by educators with whom they have a strong relationship. What can you say that would validate and express empathy for the student's experience? How can you physically demonstrate that you are listening? How can you verbally and physically respond so the student may feel less threatened?

The Issue of Respect in Trauma Responsive Schools

Much of the conflict between educators and students stems from their differing definitions of respect. Many educators define respect in terms of level and speed of compliance. Even when noncompliance is due to the students' low self-regulation skills, some educators still experience it as disrespect. In contrast, students tend to define respect in terms of how much educators recognize them as individuals and how much space educators give them to express themselves in the classroom. (See Figure 5.1 for more differences in the ways educators and students define respect.)

FIGURE 5.1
Educator Versus Student Definitions of Respect

Educator Definitions of Respect	Student Definitions of Respect
• Complying with requests promptly. • Following class rules. • Passively accepting corrections. • Accepting the classroom power hierarchy. • Not questioning the value of assignments. • Coming to class prepared with homework assignment completed properly.	• Recognizing that tumult in their home lives can make it hard for them to succeed at school. • Being allowed to help establish classroom rules. • Not being shamed and demeaned. • Having a valued voice in the classroom. • Having their efforts recognized and rewarded.

Setting and Communicating Expectations and Routines

When the goal of discipline is understood as preventing behavioral challenges, clearly communicating expectations, motivating rewards, and logical consequences are central to classroom management. It is on us as educators to ensure that

- Rules are not arbitrary but directly connected to expected classroom behaviors.
- There is no confusion among students about exactly what expected behaviors look, sound, and feel like.
- Recognitions and rewards for displaying expected behaviors are motivating to students.
- The consequences go beyond punishment and improve their ability to display expected behaviors in the future.

Too many educator–student disputes and escalated interactions stem from differing perceptions about whether a rule was broken and what the consequences are for breaking it. For example, as previously noted, educators and students may define respect differently, rendering a directive like "be respectful" subject to interpretation. It is therefore better to be more specific when crafting rules (e.g., "Use kind words when interacting with others, especially when you are upset"). Similarly, when routines are consistent throughout the day and from one day to the next, students are more likely to internalize and adhere to them. Consistent routines and expectations are important for all children, but they are particularly helpful for traumatized children, who need a school environment that counteracts the lack of predictability and safety in their home lives. The predictability of consistent routines is calming and enables students to trust that educators can create a safe environment.

Supporting Class Transitions

Educators may not fully realize the number of transitions that students make during the school day: from home to school, from an energetic breakfast period to the quiet focus of first period, from one task or subject to another while in class, then physically from the classroom to recess or lunch and back to the classroom, and many more transitions throughout the day. Each of these transitions requires refocusing from one task or subject to another, most require physical movement, and many require shifting from one educator's set of expectations to another's. Students who have low frustration tolerance and weak executive functioning skills because they are coping with trauma will struggle unless they are aided with behavioral supports.

Ineffective transitions lead to lost instructional time, and chaotic transitions create opportunities for negative interpersonal interactions among students. Many educators communicate their daily schedule and transition expectations at the beginning of the year and then spend the remainder of the year sanctioning students for not following expectations. At higher grade levels, many don't explicitly teach transition expectations on the assumption that students learned these in earlier grades.

For a transition to be organized and supported, you must have a sequenced plan for what you want students to do and explicitly teach that plan to students. You also need to have a sequenced plan for what you will say and do to prompt students immediately before the transition, during the transition, and immediately after the transition. You should have thoughtful and supported plans for at least the following four transitions:

- Transitioning students into the first period of the day and settling into learning.
- Greeting and welcoming students into your classroom at the start of each class.
- In-class transitions from one lesson or task to the next.
- Transitioning back to the classroom from recess or lunch and settling into learning.

Investing in consistency and predictability will substantially reduce the likelihood that students become dysregulated due to anxiety or uncertainty. When schedules are predictable, students can internalize the progression of tasks and activities throughout the day, making it easier for them to shift from one activity to the next. When schedules are posted, students can see what is coming up and what they've already done. This also provides you with a visual aid to point to when students have questions about the day.

Ask yourself the following questions as you reflect on, revise, and create new transition routines for students:

- What are my expectations during the transition? What behaviors and sounds do I want to see and hear?
- How am I going to communicate my expectations? What will I say and what hand signals will I use?
- Where do most students struggle? How can I precorrect to limit off-task behaviors?
- Where do students with the weakest self-regulation capacities struggle? How can I position them so they can be supported by other students with strong self-regulation skills?

Creating a Sanctuary at School

Students are better able to cope with chronic stressors and trauma when they can identify areas in their lives that are calm and orderly and can imagine and plan for a positive future (Rasmussen, Aber, & Bhana, 2004). Educators must create school environments that are distinctly different from the unsafe contexts that some students may be experiencing outside the school building and beyond the school day.

As Sandra Bloom (1995) has explained, schools can either compound students' traumas or serve as sanctuaries that build student resilience. Characteristics of schools that compound students' traumas include the following:

- Limited capacity for preventing and avoiding student confrontations.
- Inflexible behavioral routines and demands for conformity.
- Overcrowding that adds to feelings of emotional agitation and distress.
- Negative expectations for some students.
- Inconsistent and punitive discipline for displays of behavioral dysregulation.
- Poor-quality instruction and lack of academic supports.
- Visible social consequences for school failure.
- A culture that doesn't emphasize belonging.
- Educators, parents, and community members disconnected from each other.

By contrast, here are some characteristics of schools that are perceived as sanctuaries by students who are coping with trauma:

- Awareness and prevention of student confrontations.
- Empowerment of student voice and agency.
- An adequate, well-maintained space that contributes to feeling relaxed and calm.
- High expectations *and* support for all students.
- Positive, proactive, and restorative discipline.

- Rigorous instruction with varied opportunities to experience mastery.
- Private corrections to maintain student dignity.
- A culture of belonging.
- Educators, parents, and community members who are connected and mutually engaged.

Students coping with traumatic stress cannot be expected to leave their problems at the school doors and show up in the classroom ready to learn without your consistent support to bridge their transition into the learning environment.

6

Creating and Maintaining Physical Safety in the Classroom

Students coping with traumatic stressors need their schools and classrooms to be not just spaces for academic learning, but also spaces that provide them with the moments of safety and calm that every human being must experience if they are to learn how to trust themselves and others.

Physical safety is about how students experience and interact with the space around them, with one another, and with educators. We often don't realize just how much the physical design and setup of our environment affects our moods and interactions with others. In spaces that are orderly, pleasantly fragrant, and lit with warm or natural lighting, we feel more calm, comfortable, and at ease. It's therefore important to design your classroom with the intent of eliciting a *sense* of safety as well as actual safety.

Physical design of the classroom that is responsive to the needs of students coping with trauma recognizes and responds to the calming impact that one's surroundings can have by sending nonverbal signals of care and value rather than signals of threat and neglect—and by sending signals of order and organization rather than chaos and instability. For example, because trauma can rupture students' expectations of safety enough to cause internal dysregulation, they need classrooms that consider their needs for personal space, clear pathways for movement, and set-aside calming areas for preventative deescalation.

Students receive subtle signals from the physical aspects of their classroom. Consider, for example, a classroom where students' grades are posted on the wall for everyone to see. Such a setup unintentionally emphasizes individualism and competition over collectivity and collaboration. This can be emotionally threatening for students and increase their likelihood of being bullied, sending a signal that they can't trust the educator to keep them safe.

"Schools are perceived as safe when they are both free from harassment, bullying, violence, and substance use and are rich in positive, supportive relationships and interesting and rigorous opportunities for learning," write O'Malley and Amarillas (2011). There are many aspects of setting up a physically safe classroom, but I will focus here on two: aesthetics and layout.

Aesthetics

Aesthetics that attend to the needs of students coping with trauma intentionally uses color, sound, materials, nature, and other aesthetic elements to communicate a sense of welcome and safety. For example, research now shows that bright shades of orange, blue, and red can intensify negative emotions, whereas muted tones of blue, green, and purple increase feelings of calm and spaciousness (Wilms & Oberfeld, 2018).

Trauma responsive design aesthetics are also culturally responsive. Racially, ethnically, and socioeconomically marginalized students and communities are the ones that most need schools that, through their physical design and care, send the message that "those who enter here are valued and valuable." Children notice the design, cleanliness, and maintenance of their school buildings, and children from marginalized communities can internalize aspects of their schools that further confirm evidence that they are not valued members of society (Kopec & Harte, 2020). Therefore, it is important that you attend to what the aesthetics of your school and classroom communicates to the students and families it serves (Kopec & Harte, 2020).

Students need to see themselves and their communities depicted in murals, mosaics, posters, and other artifacts in and around the school, as this increases feelings of belonging. It tells students and their families that this school and classroom were planned with them in mind. Unfortunately, many schools serving marginalized communities receive limited investment in modernization and beautification, compounding students' feelings of low self-worth (Kozol, 2012).

Design Principles

Consider the following evidence-based design principles as you assess and adjust your classroom to maximize safety for all students, and especially those coping with trauma (Kopec & Harte, 2020; Ryan et al., 2014):

- Use muted shades of blue, green, and purple for a calming effect and to make a room feel more spacious.
- Keep busy color patterns and brightly colored posters to a minimum.
- Project nature videos on a back wall to provide a soothing escape for students.
- Add real or artificial plants to increase feelings of relaxation and reduce feelings of anxiety.
- If you have windows, open the blinds whenever possible to maximize natural lighting.
- Ensure that decorations are connected to students' cultural backgrounds.
- Ask students if the room feels uncomfortably cold or hot to them. Your body is often much warmer than theirs because they are smaller and seated at their desks.
- Make sure your class is free of harsh or buzzing lighting, which has been shown to increase feelings of agitation.
- If moving furniture around causes loud scraping sounds, try adding tennis balls to chair and table legs and some carpet squares or rugs.
- Ensure that the school bell is not harsh or overly loud, as this can trigger anxiety and distress.

Layout

A trauma responsive classroom needs to be a neat and orderly environment that communicates care for everyone using the space. Clutter will only increase anxiety and tax students' executive functioning skills. When organizing materials, consider whether the room is set up to facilitate student independence, such as ease of access to materials students use often. Planning for traffic patterns with the daily schedule in mind increases safety and efficient movement during transitions. Strategic placement of charts and visuals of classroom expectations can create a sense of predictability for students, as they will know exactly where to look for reminders when they need them.

In most classrooms, there will be one or two—and in some classes several—students who will need to be separated from others because they are easily distracted or are overly interactive with classmates. Such students should be given the extra space they need while maintaining their connection to the classroom community; they should not feel isolated by their seating arrangement.

Arrange desks to optimize the most common types of instructional tasks you will have students engaged in:

- Desks in rows, all facing front, is best for testing, lectures, and independent work.
- Desks in rows, side to side, is best for partner discussion.
- Desks in clusters is best for collaboration and project-based learning.
- Desks in a U-shape is best for whole-class discussions.

Desks don't have to be in traditional rows, but all chairs must face forward or at a right angle to the board so that all eyes can be focused on the front of the classroom. I have observed numerous classrooms where some students become increasingly dysregulated as the class progresses because their desks are positioned in such a way that their backs are to the board. This kind of seating unintentionally creates behavioral challenges, as these students struggle to keep up with turning to see what is being written on the board and then turning back to take notes.

Trauma is often associated with a loss of control over self and one's environment; therefore, planning the layout of your classroom to enable students to have choice over themselves and some of their classroom experiences can reduce the extent to which they feel the need to "fight" for control. Empowering students to take the lead in their learning through choice can reduce the educator frustration that results from low levels of student motivation. When students recognize and understand how to exert autonomy over some of their learning, they feel more empowered and in control, which in turn fosters motivation and a sense of responsibility for their academic success (McCombs, 2010).

Layout Principles

Consider the following evidence-based design principles as you assess and adjust your classroom to maximize safety for all students, and especially those coping with trauma (Kopec & Harte, 2020; Merrill, 2017).

Maximize signals of welcome and calm.

- Utilize the psychology of color to foster calm:
  - Muted shades of blue, green, and purple have a calming effect and make a room feel more spacious.
  - Try to avoid bright primary-colored walls that can trigger feelings of anxiety and arouse tension.
  - Reduce the amount of visual complexity from busy color patterns painted on the wall or from too many brightly colored posters.
- Utilize design based on the calming benefits of bringing nature reminders indoors:
  - Project nature videos on a back wall to provide a soothing escape for students who need a focus point that can help them destress.
  - Add (both real and artificial) plants, which increase feelings of relaxation and reduce feelings of anxiety.
  - If you have windows, open the blinds whenever possible to maximize natural lighting.
- Ensure there is a range of decor items that connect with the diversity of students' cultural backgrounds. When people see themselves and

their culture represented in the imagery and artifacts around them, their bodies release biochemicals that foster feelings of belonging.

Minimize environmental triggers.

- Does the room feel crowded with too many unnecessary items on surfaces and walls? You may need to ask a colleague and your students; you decorated your classroom, so it probably doesn't feel crowded to you.
- Is the room uncomfortably cold or hot? Ask students how they feel; your body is often much warmer than theirs because they are smaller and seated at their desks.
- Is your classroom lit with harsh or buzzing lighting that has been shown to increase feelings of agitation? A quick online search will lead you to several options for reducing the intensity of harsh lighting.
- Is there hard flooring that makes a startling sound when students move desks and chairs or drop something? Try adding tennis balls to chair and table legs and some carpet squares or rugs.
- Does your school's bell have a sharp pitch or banging sound of the type known to trigger anxiety and momentary distress? This is often an easy fix; there is no need to activate students' internal alarm systems repeatedly throughout the day.

Maximize order and organization.

- Are there clear pathways from all desks to the stations that students need to access? Many peer disagreements are fueled by students tripping over one another and their personal items.
- Are there easily identified locations for all class items? Labeled bins, boxes, and file folders make it easier for everyone.
- Do students have organizational aids to help them keep their desks uncluttered? Invest in organizers that hang on the back of students' chairs so they don't have to stuff items into messy desks.

Thoughtfully arrange seating to reduce hypervigilance.

- Students who have experienced a loss of safety are sensitive to potential threats, and many need to avoid seating options that
  - Position their back to the door. For some, the most calming seating will be near the back of the class with the ability to see their peers and the door.
  - Position them near windows. This is particularly true for students who have experienced a stray bullet hitting their home or the home of someone they know, and it may also be true for students who have experienced a weather-related disaster.
  - Position their desk in positions that force them to sit face-to-face with classmates. If using a grouped desk arrangement, try placing desks edge-to-edge in a circle or staggered off-center. Children growing up in high-stress and unsafe environments are more likely to experience the intensity of face-to face seating as distressing.
- Do a seating survey and ask students if they have preferences regarding any of these potentially triggering seating arrangements.

Attending to Equity by Considering the School Safety Needs of Students Coping with Community Violence

Violence is an ever-present threat in too many urban neighborhoods, and the number of youth shootings and homicides is traumatizing siblings, friends, and peers (Sharkey, 2010). Predictably, many of these children arrive to school with varying levels of psychological distress. However, very few are in schools that teach them how to regulate the complex cognitive, emotional, and behavioral dysregulation caused by trauma. Many schools instead respond with punitive and exclusionary discipline when these students are predictably unable to meet behavioral expectations.

These students don't have a visible wound that alerts others of their hurt and signals their need for rehabilitation. The symptoms of psychological trauma—such as intrusive thoughts, flashbacks, internal confusion, rage about what happened, and feelings of hopelessness about one's future— are not easily observable. Because the wound isn't readily visible, others may not realize their need for rehabilitative interpersonal care.

The school day for traumatized children may be filled with triggers— reminders that bring past experiences into the present, making them feel as though they are experiencing the traumatic event again. They can be triggered by a range of circumstances, such as

- Loud noises.
- Physical touch.
- Aggressive authority figures.
- Physical gestures that are perceived as threatening.
- Sudden changes in routine.
- Confusing, chaotic, or ambiguous interactions and environments.
- Anniversaries of the original event(s).

With so many triggers, students may find it difficult to follow educators' instructions, meet classroom expectations for self-management, and nego- tiate the numerous and sometimes ambiguous interpersonal interactions with educators and peers.

This is not just an individual student issue because difficulties meeting the needs of a high concentration of students coping with adversity and trauma can lead to a toxic school climate and culture that can shut down learning in the building. This is, in part, because students who have been repeatedly exposed to violence struggle to trust others, and educators who feel fearful at school may limit interactions with certain students (Chan Tack & Small, 2017; Gaylord-Harden et al., 2011; Maring & Koblinsky, 2013). In the absence of trust, the climate of a school erodes, making it harder for everyone to feel a sense of belonging (Collins, 2001).

Black youth, in particular, live in a world where authority figures abuse institutional power—they have experienced it themselves, witnessed it among family and friends, and heard credible reports of it on the news. Such abuses of power diminish their trust in authority figures and can spill over into their educational experiences.

School Safety Agents

School safety agents can either act in a threatening way, by patrolling and enforcing punishment for disciplinary infractions, or help students manage dysregulation. Research informs us that if school safety agents are just an extension of the criminal justice system, the outcomes will be especially bad for Black children (Homer & Fisher, 2020).

I have seen firsthand how safety agents can serve to primarily deescalate situations rather than escalate the conflict. For this to happen, safety agents need training to enhance their understanding of the underlying causes of students' aggressive behaviors and to equip them with developmentally appropriate practices for engaging with students in distress. In one school, this shift to prevention means that, when an educator reports a student as "having a bad day," a safety agent is there to meet that student the next morning for a breakfast check-in. This is much more effective than a protocol that places them on alert to remove the student from class the next time they act out.

Ensuring Safe Peer Interactions

In addition to setting up the physical space, having strong expectations for how students will interact with each other as they move through the space directly attends to physical safety. For example, you can reduce the likelihood of peer disputes during transitions by making the experience predictable: following a consistent set of steps and using a consistent set of cues that are reliably implemented. When you notice low-level interpersonal disputes, especially physical disagreements, during transitions, review and revise the layout of your classroom and how students have been taught to move through it. If challenges persist, ask a colleague for assistance to get a second or third opinion on your space and transition plan.

Don't ignore low-level verbal aggression such as teasing, bossing, belittling and abusive statements, sarcasm, and threats. Students will only rely on their educators to assist with interpersonal disputes if they think they can trust their educators to see, recognize, and respond to all forms of aggression. It is when small acts of interpersonal harm are ignored that serious violence can erupt. Escalating aggression, bullying, and fighting in a school are signs that students don't trust the adults in the building to intervene and provide safety, so they're taking matters into their own hands.

Many educators are unaware of just how unsafe many students feel at school (Biag, 2014; Schwab-Stone et al., 1995). StopBullying.gov reports that fewer than 20 percent of bullying acts are reported to adults, one in four students will experience bullying during the academic year, and 160,000 students miss school each day for fear of bullying. They define bullying as unwanted, aggressive behavior that involves a real or perceived power imbalance. Research also clearly shows that feeling unsafe at school compromises students' abilities to learn (Lacoe, 2020).

When responding to peer aggression, be sure to show care for both the victim and the aggressor. Demonstrate care for the victim by swiftly shutting down the aggressive behavior and ensuring that it does not continue. Demonstrate care for the aggressor by trying to understand what underlying issues have led them to consider aggression and then teach an alternative prosocial response.

Some students get away with being aggressive toward others by joking about harmful actions or making sarcastic and demeaning comments. Others covertly engage in low-level acts of violence in the hallway, unsupervised bathrooms and stairwells, or lunch and recess periods. Becoming aware of the extent to which students feel unsafe at your school and in your classroom is critical to facilitating physical safety. It is important to note that this awareness cannot be understood through the eyes of the adults in the building; it must be based on feedback from students.

In many classrooms, educators let low-level verbal and physical aggression slide so they can get through their lesson plan. However, this only emboldens the aggressor while causing the victim either to withdraw from learning or to fight back. Students are strongly motivated to be accepted as part of a peer community, so if you can respond to aggression in ways that teach prosocial ways of managing and communicating strong emotions, you have a chance of creating lasting change.

Types of Intentional Aggression

There are four main types of intentional aggression:

Verbal aggression involves name calling, threats, and other disrespectful comments to create a power imbalance. Playful teasing can begin as mutual and become aggressive when it persists despite at least one person expressing the desire for it to stop.

Social or relational aggression relies on interpersonal exclusion and manipulation to hurt others and can include gossip and spreading rumors. This can be very difficult for adults to observe and catch, and it can be equally hard for students to verbally express what they are experiencing.

Cyberaggression is the use of the internet and cellphones to embarrass, harass, or threaten others. This is quickly becoming the most prevalent and harmful form of aggression and is insidious because it can be difficult to identify the perpetrators.

Physical aggression includes taking and breaking things in addition to hitting, kicking, tripping, and pushing. This is the easiest form of aggression to identify, but it is often preceded by the other forms of aggression.

Planned Responses

Too many educators pretend not to notice aggression because they are uncertain how to respond or concerned that they may unintentionally escalate the conflict. It is incorrect to assume that the aggressor will grow out of it or to believe that the victim needs to learn how to stand up for themselves. The best way for you to manage uncertainty about how to respond to aggressive behaviors is to have a planned response that is both nonescalating and instructive.

Planned responses are preconceived, emotionally neutral instructional responses to predictable or frequently occurring behaviors. When targeting aggressive behaviors, planned responses must

- Signal that the behavior must stop.
- Remind the student of a replacement behavior.
- Recognize and validate the student for exhibiting the desired behavior.

Here are five steps to planning your response to aggressive student behaviors:

1. Identify the undesired behavior.
2. Determine the nonverbal sign and short phrase you will use to signal to the student that their current behavior must stop. Teach this phrase to students. Use it by first making eye contact and then signaling or speaking to the student. When possible, move closer to the student to use proximity control to get them to stop the undesired behavior. When using verbal corrections, avoid public shaming.
3. Identify a desired replacement behavior (e.g., "Keep your hands to yourselves while walking to the door," "Immediately return the items that you took"). Teach the replacement behavior and have students practice it.
4. Determine the nonverbal signal and verbal statement you will use to remind students of the replacement behavior. Teach the signal and statement to students.
5. Identify several nonverbal and verbal ways that you can acknowledge and affirm students as soon as they stop the aggressive behavior and demonstrate the replacement behavior.

7

Building Pedagogically Caring Relationships

Relationships are critical to the process of creating safety, and experiencing safety is foundational to the trust needed for strengthening and maintaining relationships. Together, safety and relationships are external supports that educators can provide to reduce the negative effects of trauma on and build resilience in students.

Resilience is the capacity to withstand stress while maintaining functional health across many life domains. It is critical for reducing the intergenerational transmission of disadvantage (Garmezy, 1993; Schetter & Dolbier, 2011). Too often, discussions of resilience focus on internal psychological and emotional attributes such as self-esteem, executive functioning, adaptive coping, and internal locus of control (Cederblad et al., 1994; Ryff & Singer, 2003). But research shows that these attributes are only as strong as the relational supports that facilitate the development of resilience during and after exposure to traumatic stressors (Echterling et al., 2005; National Scientific Council on the Developing Child (2015). These resilience-building social supports are the focus of this chapter.

The fact that relational supports are foundational to healing from trauma seems self-evident enough, but exactly what relational supports are can be unclear (Rak & Patterson, 1996; Woodward & Joseph, 2003). Relational supports include consistent, caring, responsive, and reciprocal interpersonal interactions between children and their family, peers, and adults. Unfortunately, research shows that children coping with trauma are often left adrift without these supports. For example, one study found that children coping with interpersonal trauma such as sexual and physical abuse and witnessing domestic violence often lack a caring connection with their educators (Dods, 2013). This is largely because their acting-out behaviors push educators away—even though those same students report that they act out so that someone will respond to their needs.

Educator–student relationships affect academic achievement and student self-regulation skills, and positive relationships are associated with a greater likelihood of making it to graduation (Goodenow & Grady, 1993; Klem & Connell, 2004; Ma, 2003). In fact, these relationships are so critical that they are now included as a component of rigorous pedagogy (Liew et al., 2010; Roorda et al., 2011; Wentzel, 1997). Strong bonds between students and educators are also associated with a lower likelihood that students will engage in criminal and violent behaviors, abuse drugs and alcohol, get pregnant as an adolescent, or suffer emotional distress (Smith, n.d.).

Because relationship building is rarely taught during preservice training, many educators approach it as something certain people are just good at while others aren't. Understanding and depersonalizing student resistance can help to change this fixed mindset about relationship building.

Students with histories of harmful or neglectful relationships have trouble accepting relationship building as genuine, expressing their appreciation of it, and reciprocating in healthy ways (Mihalas et al., 2009). However, when asked, these students report that they value their educators' caring actions, particularly attentiveness and active listening. The challenge is that due to their experiences distrusting adults, they will often test their educators' efforts—a coping response that may be maladaptive at school but adaptive in other contexts they must navigate.

Building relationships with these students takes time, consistency, and persistence. Some may respond positively quite quickly, whereas others may take more time to let their guard down. Thankfully, research helps us better understand students' perspectives and the relationship-building efforts that traumatized students most appreciate (Dods, 2013):

- Students coping with trauma need educators to lead interactions—to intuit their need for connections, initiate conversation, and invite students to connect with them.
- Students are sensitive to authenticity and are most likely to discern it when educators actively listen to what they are saying, show an understanding attitude toward their difficulties, and validate their distress.
- Students exhibiting off-task behaviors need educators who are attuned to their overt and covert cues of distress and are able to respond in ways that are developmentally supportive.
- Students who have learned to mistrust adults need educators who approach them as individuals, such as by asking about things that are personally meaningful and committing to sustaining the relationship over time.

Educators in schools with a high rate of trauma exposure often express the impossibility of building strong bonds with "so many needy students." This is because, as Kristen Souers and Pete Hall (2016) have noted, many educators perceive traumatized students as bottomless wells of emotional need, and themselves as the only saviors who can fill those wells to capacity. However, emotion-focused relationship building is completely unsustainable if large numbers of students in a school or classroom are coping with high levels of trauma.

Educator–Student Relationships and Pedagogical Care

I am asking you to develop educator–student relationships that are undergirded by an ethic of pedagogical care (Mihalas et al., 2009). This means demonstrating care for students through everyday interactions, such as during whole-class and individual instruction, while providing behavioral and academic corrections, and during informal interactions like walking in the hallway.

Building caring pedagogical relationships with students is dramatically different from building *friendships*. A few of the relationships that you build with students may become enduring emotional friendships, but *all* your educator–student relationships can be pedagogically caring. Attempting to develop close emotional relationships with all students is unsustainable and bound to fail, causing relational withdrawal and harming students.

One educator with whom I worked discussed the sudden loss of safety that students experience when educators who have poured themselves into their students leave in the middle of the school year or don't return in the fall because of burnout. She stated that students feel betrayed and experience "emotional panic" at the loss of relational support from someone who convinced them that it would be safe to feel and express their vulnerabilities. In response to this loss of safety, students become emotionally dysregulated, escalate their acting-out behaviors, are punitively sanctioned by the school, and ultimately increase the height of their trust barrier with the next educator who attempts to develop a caring relationship with them.

Consistency of presence is necessary for caring relationships to be safe. Your aim should be to create caring pedagogical relationships that are

- Emotional enough to communicate feelings of warmth.
- Safe enough for students to trust that they will not be rejected when they make mistakes.
- Friendly enough for students to believe that their educator is happy to have them in the classroom.
- Resilient enough to withstand relational repair when relationship-damaging actions occur.
- Sustainable enough to last through countless educator–student interactions across the academic year.

In these kinds of relationships, educators

- Express genuine curiosity about each individual student.
- Adapt their teaching based on their awareness of who students are.
- Maintain present-moment awareness of students' emotional states.
- Communicate their belief in students' abilities to reach high expectations.

Attending to Equity in Relationship Building

It is important to focus on building relationships with students who we may initially view as different from ourselves. The truth is that even among those who strongly endorse principles of racial equality, unconscious feelings of superiority, discomfort, anxiety, and fear can get in the way as they try to build authentic relationships with members of marginalized groups (Stanley et al., 2011; Sue, 2010). In the classroom, the responsibility for bridging cultural barriers lies with the educator, who holds the power to broaden or limit the opportunities that students have to bring their whole selves to school (Milner, 2006).

Differences between educators and students in status characteristics, such as race, ethnicity, socioeconomic background, and immigration history, are often associated with differences in life experiences that can create moments of cultural incongruence. Such differences can lead to moments of misunderstanding or unintended slights. No educator is exempt from the need to get comfortable with having uncomfortable conversations to uncover and bridge points of disconnection. For example, you may have race, ethnicity, and class background in common with a given student, but there may be other differences, such as gender identification or sexual orientation.

Sometimes learning about others, especially when there is a power differential, means taking on the responsibility of creating a safe environment that allows for uncomfortable conversations. You can start such conversations by asking students and their family members to help you understand why they behave or respond in ways that are different from what you expected or why they have a perception about something that you didn't intend. The following tips can get you started:

- Listen to understand rather than to respond.
- Show vulnerability to help others open up.
- Reserve judgment about what you are learning from others.
- Be patient and show appreciation.
- Admit when you get it wrong and be willing to make adjustments.

Poverty Law Center (2019) offers a guide for having dif-
.ions with students called "Let's Talk!"—you can find it
oɪɪ..

Take the vulnerable step of engaging in critical self-reflection about
the students with whom you have neutral or negative relationships. Ask
yourself at least the following two questions and sit with the discomfort
of your honest answers:

**What are the racial, ethnic, gender, immigrant, disability status,
and other characteristics of the students with whom you have
neutral or negative relationships?** It is likely you will have the strongest
relationships with the students who have racial, ethnic, gender, socioeconomic, and cultural backgrounds that closely align with yours. This
can start the intentional process of reflecting on your biases to determine
how to bridge the gap.

**Are the students you discipline the most also the ones with whom
you have neutral or negative relationships?** Punitive discipline breaks
relational bonds. Unless intentional work is done to repair the relationship, it will get worse over the course of the academic year. Students who
believe that they are disliked by their educators are more likely to exhibit
dysregulated behaviors and less motivated to follow classroom rules.

Relationship Stage Framework

Psychologist Clay Cook and colleagues (2018) developed the Establish-
Maintain-Restore (EMR) relationship stage framework for matching
relationship-building strategies to different student needs. I extend this
framework by adding a "Pre-establish" stage. By assessing whether you
are in the pre-establish, establish, maintain, or restore stage with each
student, you will be able to identify the appropriate relationship-building
strategies to use.

The Pre-establish Stage

In this stage, you and the student have had a pattern of conflictual interactions that have laid a foundation of negative emotions and mistrust.

During this stage, you must monitor and break old patterns of inter-actions. The goal is to identify negative interaction patterns, acknowl-edge the need to establish positive patterns, and then take action. During this stage, it is important to acknowledge and plan for the high likelihood that the student may reject initial attempts to improve the relationship.

Relationship building is only sustainable when you are able to show compassion for yourself and your students. You can demonstrate com-passion by showing students that they don't have to earn your kindness. A resentful educator prioritizes their need to be right, but a compassionate educator prioritizes maintaining student dignity (Souers & Hall, 2016).

If you are trying to establish relationships with a student who is not immediately receptive, consider the 2-by-10 strategy: Spend two minutes a day over ten consecutive school days working to build trust with that student. The consistency of the interaction matters more than the length of time. The student's feelings of relational safety will increase with each consecutive interaction. These brief but caring interactions should focus on showing students that you see them as individuals, that you value get-ting to know their interests and strengths, and that you see something positive in them and are able to affirm it. Try any of the following forms of interaction (and many more):

- A brief, lighthearted conversation in the hallway before the student enters the classroom.
- Stopping to help the student as you circulate during independent work time.
- A brief conversation with the student while escorting the class to the cafeteria.
- A short encouraging discussion after the final bell.

Many educators believe that big generous acts are needed to build positive relationships when conflict or distrust exists. For example, one educator I know was planning a special lunch to "start new" with a dis-ruptive student. The educator was anxious about whether the student would receive the lunch well. This special lunch was too high stakes; if it failed, the relationship would be set back even further. By contrast, the 2-by-10 strategy is a low-stakes intervention. Some educators plan a time in their lesson plans when the class is engaged in individual work to strategically spend a little extra time with each of the target students. The interaction must be authentic. It could begin with a compliment or question about something you observed. The purpose is to demonstrate that you want to know the student as an individual.

Relationship building is a high-value investment opportunity—the one aspect of students' school experiences that can be fundamentally changed by a single educator. As Jason Okonofua, a psychology professor who examines the benefits of empathic discipline, has noted, "Just having one better relationship with a teacher at school—just one—can serve as a buffer for all the other struggles and challenges at school" (quoted in Sparks, 2016).

The Establish Stage

In this stage, you and the student have a neutral relationship, having not yet laid a foundation of trust. During this stage, you are implementing pedagogical relationship-building strategies with all students. This enables students to feel safe, connected, and respected, which strengthens their motivation to engage their self-regulation skills.

By sharing a common environment for many hours a day, several days a week, and many months a year, educators and students are in a relationship, and every interaction either hinders or strengthens the relationship. Educators who are drowning in the impossibility of creating close emotional connections through interactions that occur outside instructional time can shift their perspective to building relationships through classroom interactions.

Starting each day with a genuine and welcoming greeting at the door is one small way to ensure that their first interaction with you each day is positive. Feelings of belonging in the school and classroom are strongly tied to academic investment (Allday & Pakurar, 2007). Greeting students at the door is also a way to quickly check their mood and well-being as they enter the room—vital preventative information for managing potential behavior challenges. Stand at, near, or outside the door to cheerfully welcome students into the classroom—each one, by name. Consider adding an individualized greeting for each student, such as a special handshake, high-five, or side-hug.

If the student was disciplined the previous day, or if they are returning from a detention or suspension, a gracious hello that includes a word of gratitude is an effective reset. Examples include

- "It's good to see you. Welcome to a new day."
- "We missed you! I'm glad our class is complete again."
- "We are doing group work today. It's good to have you with us."

Show interest in students' lives outside your class by being genuinely curious about them as individuals, affirming their many nonacademic strengths, thanking them for the specific talents they contribute to your classroom community, and complimenting them on special achievements and important life events such as participation in sports, drama, music, or other extracurricular activities.

Only by knowing who your students are will you be able to fully engage them in learning. This means asking classroom questions that invite them to share about their home lives, their interests, and their likes and dislikes. When it comes to school experiences, it means going beyond academics and genuinely inquiring about their perspectives on whether school is going well for them. Ask them where they experience joy and engagement and where they experience anxiety, avoidance, and self-doubt.

Interest surveys give students the opportunity to share more about themselves with you. Use these surveys to learn more about students' experiences both in and out of school. They are most effective when first building relationships, at either the beginning of the year or the beginning of each new semester. The surveys shouldn't be very long; a few

.ime spread over the academic year is better than one long start of the year. Here are some possible questions to ask:

- Tell me about something you love doing that has nothing to do with school.
- What is one of your favorite things to do on the weekend?
- What is one thing that your teachers don't know about you?
- What are the top three classes that you have ever enjoyed in school?
- What is the class that you have liked the least?
- What is one thing that you know a lot about and still want to know much more about?
- What is one thing that you know a little about and want to know much more about?
- What is one thing that you know almost nothing about and want to know much more about?
- What is something you think some teachers "don't get" about students your age?
- What is something that's been hard for you in your life?
- What is something about yourself that makes you feel proud?
- What is one thing that always makes you smile?
- What do you think makes a good teacher?
- How do you think teachers should respond when a student is not following the rules?
- What are a couple questions you have about me?

Developing a personalized understanding is a two-way street. Your students also need to know who you are, beyond your role as their educator. Educators who are willing and brave enough to share who they are with their students are better able to find points of authentic connection. This is particularly important when educators and students differ in terms of race, ethnicity, socioeconomic status, or immigration history. Build authentic relationships by asking questions and using assignments that enable students to share their stories, and by weaving stories of your life into instruction.

The idea of taking time to establish personal relationships with multiple students can seem overwhelming, but it need not be so. A quick sticky note to a few students at a time can communicate to the entire class you care and see them as individuals. Use technology to your advantage: many schools have student and parent messenger communication platforms that can be used for brief two-way communication. Journaling allows students to get valuable ungraded writing practice while also providing a window into who they are as individuals (Regan, 2003).

Listen for students' verbal and nonverbal indicators of distress. When you have strong relationships with your students, they can receive comments such as "I see that something is wrong, and I am here if you need to talk" as authentic acknowledgment of their troubles. For many students, this authentic acknowledgment is all they need from their classroom teacher when it comes to discussing the details of their traumas.

The Maintain Stage

In this stage, you are strengthening the good-enough relationships that you have established by intentionally striving for a 5-to-1 ratio of positive praise to behavioral corrections or critique. As Clay Cook and colleagues (2018) note, established relationships often diminish over time because educators ignore or miss opportunities to reinforce good behavior and unintentionally pay more attention to negative behavior.

The fact is that inappropriate student behavior is predictive of educator reprimands, but appropriate behavior is not predictive of educator praise. Frequently receiving behavioral corrections but not recognition only serves to perpetuate negative behavior. Thankfully, this cycle can be broken by enforcing a 5-to-1 ratio of positive to corrective comments.

You can provide students with positive feedback for all sorts of reasons: following directions, displaying engagement, staying on task, answering questions correctly, and so on. Praise should be tailored to each specific student and account for factors like age and skill level. Noncontingent affirmations such as a smile and nod at random intervals can also help increase the ratio of positives to negatives, especially for students who

.orrective redirections. Positive affirmations increase ...steem, improve their relationships with others, and help them ... ...ected to the school community, all factors that mitigate the effects of traumatic stress.

There are three primary types of praise:

- **Personal praise** such as "You are really smart!" tends to focus on natural talents or skills that come easily to students, rather than the effort they put in or the techniques they use. Minimize use of this type of praise.
- **Effort-based praise** such as "You worked really hard to minimize rounding errors on this assignment" emphasizes what students can control as they attempt to get better at a task or learning goal. Maximize this type of praise, especially for struggling learners.
- **Behavior-specific praise** such as "You did a great job transitioning into the classroom and getting your homework into the homework folder right away" lets students know what they are doing correctly. This is an evidence-based classroom management strategy that focuses on providing specific feedback to show your approval of student behavior. Maximize this type of praise for all students.

Try the "paperclips in your pocket" tracking method to attain the 5-to-1 ratio of positive to corrective feedback. Place one red and five green paperclips in one pocket. When you make a corrective statement, transfer the red paperclip to a second pocket. You then need to transfer all five green paperclips from the first pocket to the second one by making one positive statement for each before you can make another corrective statement. Positive statements include positively worded behavioral directions that tell students what to do rather than what they shouldn't do.

Here are 15 genuine affirming statements that you can say to students, adapted from the *Big Life Journal* blog (Eidens, 2022).

- You really hung in there by _____.
- It was nice to see you _____.
- You pushed yourself today, and it paid off.
- I was so impressed today when you _____.

- It was awesome to see you _____.
- I hope you feel proud about _____, because you should.
- It's not easy to _____, but you are making it happen.
- Congratulations for _____.
- That's a great question.
- That was a really good choice.
- I noticed when you _____.
- Your hard work will pay off.
- I see that you are trying hard and doing your best.
- Keep trying—you will get it!
- It's exciting to see you get better at _____.

Remember that positive feedback also applies to communication with students' family members. Caregivers can become frustrated with repeated messages home if they highlight student misbehavior without offering suggestions for support. When parents or guardians perceive that their child is not being cared for by adults in the school, an adversarial relationship can develop. Consider as well whether family members have themselves been treated poorly by educators in the past; such experiences could make them reluctant to collaborate with school staff. Like your relationships with students, relationships with family members must be developed and maintained over time.

The Restore Stage

At some point each year, every educator will need to do some work to restore relationships that have been harmed, whether by student behaviors or by the educator's shaming corrections. Much of the work of restoring relationships relies on the educator's mindset or approach and their ability to provide coregulation supports to the student.

Research shows that holding a restorative mindset makes the emotional labor of supporting students who exhibit dysregulated behavior lighter, thus protecting your emotional and psychological well-being (Chang & Davis, 2009; Hargreaves, 2000). When there is a breakdown in the educator–student relationship, take active steps to communicate that you want to understand and validate the student's perspective even if it is different from your own (Cook et al., 2018).

Empathy statements are short phrases that help create trust and mutual understanding by using words to communicate that you care about and are interested in understanding students' experiences and perceptions. Delivering an empathy statement takes imagination because it can be difficult to see another's perspective, especially in a stressful situation. Delivering statements that communicate empathy is not necessarily about agreeing with the student's perspective, but about validating their right to have feelings and perspectives that may differ from yours. One empathetic statement from a caring adult can go a long way toward enriching a student's feelings of school belonging. Follow these steps to deliver an empathy statement:

1. **Assess the situation.** Let the student know that you care about understanding their situation and their perspective by asking questions such as these:
   - "Would you please tell me more about what is happening/what you think happened?"
   - "I can see that you are upset. Can you tell me more about how you are feeling?"
   - "I heard that _____ happened; can you tell me more about that?"
2. **Clarify the situation** to reduce the likelihood that the student will get frustrated as they try to explain themselves. Consider using these prompts:
   - "I want to make sure I understand what you're telling me. I'm hearing that _____."
   - "Please correct me if I am wrong. I think _____ happened."
   - "What I hear you saying is _____. Is that correct? Is there anything I am missing?"
3. **Validate their feelings** with statements such as these:
   - "That sounds frustrating/upsetting/hurtful."
   - "I can see why you are upset/angry/sad."
   - "That must have been a difficult experience."

4. **Share what you experienced and how you feel** with statements such as these:
   - "I feel _____ when students _____."
   - "It is hard for me to _____ when students _____."
   - "I get _____ when students _____."

5. **Reassure students that you are both in this together** by using "we" statements to indicate the actions they can take to move forward:
   - "We can work together to help you _____."
   - "We can create a _____ so that you can _____."
   - "We can go together to talk with _____ about _____."

Understanding How Students Feel About You

It is important to determine how students perceive their relationship with you. Obtaining student feedback is crucial to relationship-building. It is possible to think you're doing everything right and still get it wrong if you do not check in with your students. Consider designing a quick survey that can serve as an exit ticket at the end of a class period. Ask whether students

- Feel respected by the adults in the building.
- See educators as supportive and caring.
- Believe that educators understand their problems outside school.
- Experience discipline as fair or feel singled out.
- Think of instruction as connected to their identities and interests.
- Think that educators recognize, value, and reward their efforts.

Without the persistence of caring educators who consistently engage in relationship-building strategies, students are left to rely on their under-developed interpersonal coping skills. You can utilize your responses to students' dysregulated behaviors as opportunities to teach them the skills needed to build and maintain healthy relationships. Teaching them how to do differently and giving them opportunities to practice those new behaviors is one of the strongest ways to ensure accountability.

8

Providing Psychologically Safe Discipline

Psychological safety means protection from derogatory statements that damage one's sense of self. When students who exhibit dysregulated behaviors are disciplined, they need to hear that their behavior needs to change, concrete suggestions for how to improve, and that they are valued regardless of the behaviors they display. Too often, the discipline process hinders students' sense of self-worth (Bordovskaia & Baeva, 2015). Discipline builds accountability when it balances enforcement of rules with empathy for students' well-being.

Coregulation

When we meet students' dysregulated behaviors with coregulation—consistently calming, regulating responses—they learn how to self-regulate their thinking, emotions, and behaviors. Coregulation includes three components (Rosanbalm & Murray, 2017):

- Cultivating a warm, responsive relationship by displaying care and affection.
- Structuring the environment to make self-regulation manageable by avoiding vague behavioral expectations, unclear guidance during transitions, and prolonged quiet seated work time.
- Coaching—modeling, instruction, opportunities for practice, and positive reinforcement of even modest progress.

See Figure 8.1 for more information on how to make sure the above criteria are met.

Coregulation is also a deescalation strategy because it defuses and brings down the emotional intensity of the experience and interaction. By modeling calm self-regulated behavior in the low tone of your voice and neutral body posture, you are actively teaching students what they can reflect back to you to demonstrate calm, self-regulated behavior. It also provides you with a concrete alternative to saying, "Calm or cool down," which is often unhelpful and sometimes triggering. You can say something like "Bring your voice down and talk like I'm talking," "Take deeper breaths and breathe like I'm breathing," or "Slow down and walk like I'm walking." Your ability to respond to acting-out behaviors with coregulation will improve over time and will become easier as your relationships with students become stronger.

Attending to Equity by Holding Yourself Accountable for Discipline

In far too many classrooms, students from historically marginalized groups are scapegoated in misguided attempts to manage acting-out behaviors, singled out to discourage other students from acting the same way (Price, 2006). This often occurs when educators with poor classroom management skills and anxiety about losing control are faced with managing a classroom of diverse students.

Here's how veteran educator Verna Price (2006) describes it. An educator will choose one student, typically a Black male, and use him as an example to show how much "power" the educator has. The educator publicly confronts the student; publicly questions his ability; disciplines him punitively, as an example to others; and continues the public confrontation until the student explodes emotionally, escalates the discipline issue, or refuses to engage academically. It usually ends with the educator writing up a behavior referral and having him removed from the classroom.

FIG...
Coregulation Strategies

Strategy	Elementary School	Middle School	High School
Building a Warm, Responsive Relationship	• Be consistently positive • Provide support and empathy in times of distress • Validate emotional experiences • Respond to developmental needs		
Structuring the Environment	• Provide time and space to relax and calm down • Clarify rules and consequences • Scaffold complex academic, behavioral, and social situations	• Provide time and space to relax and calm down • Monitor for risk-taking behaviors • Establish rules and consequences that incentivize good behavior	• Provide time and space to relax and calm down • Limit opportunities for risk taking • Establish rules and consequences that incentivize good behavior • Collaborate to identify supportive environments
Coaching	• Model conflict resolution • Provide self-calming strategies • Teach students ways to relax • Encourage positive self-talk • Demonstrate interpersonal flexibility	• Model goal setting • Teach problem solving • Provide stress management strategies • Help students manage time • Promote good organization and forward planning	• Model complex decision making and problem solving • Teach healthy relationship skills • Provide stress management strategies • Promote long-term goal setting

Research shows that racial and gender disparities in who receives punitive discipline are largely accounted for by educators' perceptions rather than actual disparities in behavior (Skiba et al., 2002). Educators are more likely to send Black and Latinx students than White students to the office for the same disciplinary infraction, and Black and Latinx students are more likely than White students to receive punitive punishments (Okonofua & Eberhardt, 2015). Stereotypes can lead educators to see particular behaviors as more concerning when coming from Black students versus White students, and especially coming from Black boys (Okonofua et al., 2016). A vicious cycle is thus initiated, because Black and Latinx students notice this disciplinary difference and may respond negatively in ways that increase their likelihood of acting out.

Personal acknowledgment, reflection, and accountability can enable you to keep implicit biases from determining who experiences psychologically safe discipline:

Acknowledgment. You must ensure that your classroom does not replicate the racial, ethnic, and gender biases that permeate much of our social world. This means acknowledging that race, ethnicity, and gender matter when it comes to discipline (Staats, 2014).

Reflection. Examine your data to determine the racial and/or gender disparities related to discipline in your classroom. Take time to understand students' stories: Are you sanctioning them for having a different culture or lifestyle from you? Identify the things you do that perpetuate challenging interactions. As Carolyn Holbrook (2006) notes, "Taking a look at the parts of ourselves that we don't want to face can be uncomfortable. However, when you are responsible for children's lives, this kind of honesty is vital" (p. 120).

Accountability. All educators must hold themselves accountable for any racial and gender disparities in the discipline they mete out. If you find such disparities, debrief with a colleague and ask them to observe your classroom to help you understand how to take corrective action.

Implementing Trauma Responsive Discipline

Maintaining order and adhering to behavioral expectations need not come at the expense of students having a positive sense of themselves. Disciplinary interactions need to reassure students that they are being held accountable because they are valued members of the school community. Trauma responsive discipline both prioritizes students' dignity and strengthens their self-regulation, enabling you to meet students' needs for psychological safety while managing the classroom effectively and minimizing lost instructional time.

Children coping with traumatic stressors often have intense emotional reactions to rules and discipline and may push back with inappropriate acting-out behaviors. These behaviors may stem from their immature attempts to gain a sense of safety by exerting control; if you respond with anger and punitive sanctions, they may end up feeling more unsafe and display more acting-out behaviors, perpetuating a vicious cycle.

Positively Stated Rules and Corrections

You can reduce the amount of pushback you receive from students by ensuring that classroom rules are clear and focused on what students *should* do rather than on what they should not do. Positively stated rules and corrections implicitly communicate to students that you believe in their desire and ability to meet your expectations.

Behavioral corrections can be delivered indirectly by affirming students who are demonstrating the desired behavior. By saying "Thank you, Jamal, for ___" or "Good job, Jasmine, with ___," you also remind students who are not exhibiting those behaviors about your expectations. When students receive appropriate support to successfully follow classroom rules, their self-worth increases and they are more likely to be engaged learners. Be sure to explicitly teach and reteach expectations and to provide verbal and nonverbal reminders.

Review your class rules to see if they follow these guiding principles:

- **The expected behavior is clearly stated.** "Stay focused on the assigned task during independent work time" is better than "No talking during independent work time."
- **The expected behavior is clearly observable.** "Gather all needed materials at the start of the class" is better than "Be responsible."
- **Language is developmentally appropriate.** For younger students, "Use kind words" is better than "Be considerate of others."

And here are a few additional dos and don'ts to consider:

- *Do* keep your behavioral requests brief and limited to one task or objective at a time. Once the student has complied, you can make the next behavioral request. A student who appears to be noncompliant may simply have trouble staying focused and organized to follow multi-step requests.
- *Don't* be vague. Simply saying "Get your work done!" is not very helpful, especially if the student has behavioral and self-regulation challenges.
- *Do* make sure that your behavioral requests are connected to classroom and school rules.
- *Do* let students know why the behavioral request matters. If the student resists or asks why they should follow your behavioral request, have a short and simple rationale prepared.
- *Don't* follow your behavioral requests with excessive justifications. Long, drawn-out explanations can cause students to lose focus on what you are asking them to do.
- *Do* state your behavioral requests in a matter-of-fact, emotionally neutral tone. Using a tone of voice that is demanding, sarcastic, or angry only invites resistance.
- *Do* state your behavioral requests as polite directives. Ensuring that you are always polite in your requests models the behaviors that you want students to display to you and to one another.

- *Don't* state your behavioral requests as questions unless there is a real opportunity for students to exercise choice.
- *Do* give students time to comply. Simply wait quietly and remain near the student without hovering in an aggressive or threatening manner. Give the student 5 to 15 seconds, depending on the request and the students' emotional state. Do not repeat or elaborate on your request until the 5 to 15 seconds have elapsed.
- *Do* make sure students follow through and comply with your request, then affirm them for doing so.

Precorrections

Precorrections allow you to take a proactive approach to discipline. They are strategically planned, short, direct prompts that state expectations. They are given before and during activities that can lead to off-task behaviors. Precorrections work as whole-class, small-group, or individual behavioral supports. When using with a small group or individual student, make sure to communicate precorrections away from the rest of the class.

Precorrections help students remember the many expectations they encounter throughout the day, which can be especially challenging for students who are struggling with self-regulation. By increasing the likelihood that students will successfully meet behavioral expectations, precorrections reduce disciplinary interactions and augment students' sense of school belonging.

Trauma responsive discipline does not shame students or base corrections in any way on student identity. An identity-based statement like "You are so disruptive when you blurt out the answers" tells students that they are disruptive people. Many children coping with trauma have experienced a lot of shame and are quick to internalize negative messages about who they are.

The alternative is to provide task-focused behavioral corrections that state and restate the behaviors you want to see. So, for example, for the student who blurts out answers, a task-focused correction might go something like this: "Please raise your hand and wait for me to select someone.

Now, I am going to ask another question. Please wait for me to select a student to answer." If the misbehavior is recurring, use a precorrection before the student has time to display it ("I am going to ask some questions; please wait for me to select a student to answer").

Relational Discipline

Task-focused behavioral corrections preserve your ability to use relational discipline, which research shows is more effective for gaining compliance than negative or punitive consequences (Marzano, Marzano, & Pickering, 2003). Educators who effectively use relational discipline value strengthening student voice, developing social and emotional competencies, and preserving student dignity while correcting behaviors.

When you respond to acting-out behaviors in ways that promote safety, you are making space for the possibility that there is more going on than what you can see on the surface. The goal is threefold: stop the undesired behavior, express care, and redirect the student toward the replacement behavior. The relational response is in sharp contrast to punitive discipline, which is based on the belief that fear, shame, or discomfort associated with a negative consequence are effective preventative measures. But punitive discipline only produces temporary compliance and does little to motivate long-term change.

When practicing relational discipline, use this graduated sequence of behavioral corrections that don't create feelings of shame or threat:

- Make extended eye contact with the student exhibiting acting-out behavior. This is a subtle, powerful way of alerting them to the fact that you see them and their behavior needs correcting.
- Make eye contact, then use a physical sign, like a finger to the lips, to indicate the behavior that needs to change. This is most effective when you follow that gesture with another that indicates what you want them to do as a replacement behavior.
- If the student still isn't following instructions, provide a short reminder of what they should be doing, as privately and subtly as

possible. This provides them with a behavioral prompt without the defensiveness that comes from feeling publicly shamed.

- You also have the option of reminding the whole class of the expected appropriate behavior while giving the off-task student time to self-correct.

Relational discipline works best when you are secure about your position of authority in the classroom, because you don't feel the need to use fear to keep students from acting out and are more likely to accept that consequences can wait until you or the student are less agitated. There are many drawbacks to delivering immediate consequences:

- It is hard to be thoughtful about consequences when you need to get back to teaching the class.
- Decisions are more likely to be emotional rather than empirical.
- You run the risk of making a threat that you can't carry out.
- You don't have time to anticipate how parents or administrators will react to the consequence.
- The interaction is less likely to be a learning opportunity for the student.

An Instructional Approach to Discipline

Just as we are trained to respond to academic errors with increased instruction and guidance, we must respond to behavioral errors by identifying the missing social and emotional skills and then teaching and reteaching those skills. Using behavioral errors as teaching opportunities is at the heart of an instructional approach to discipline (Madigan et al., 2016).

Pedagogical responses to off-task behaviors aim to ensure that students leave each discipline interaction having learned something that can help them meet your behavioral expectations in the future; each discipline interaction becomes a learning experience. Instructional discipline is grounded in the Positive Behavioral Interventions and Supports (PBIS) model, which frames acting out as behavioral errors (i.e., as learning opportunities).

State, explain, and model expected behaviors, then give students the chance to practice them with supervision. Reteach, rehearse, practice, and give positive feedback to reinforce the expected behavior until it becomes a student habit or routine. As with academic instruction, scaffold students' learning and differentiate your responses based on their individual learning needs. (See Figure 8.2 for a comparison of instructional versus punitive corrections.)

One way to teach behavioral skills to students on an ongoing basis is to set aside a few minutes each class for brief social and emotional learning lessons. Whatever behavior challenge you observe that day becomes the behavior teaching lesson for tomorrow. This approach takes to heart the understanding that the best way to respond to misbehavior is to use it as a teaching opportunity.

FIGURE 8.2

Instructional Versus Punitive Approach to Corrections

Instructional Discipline	Punitive Discipline
• The educator points out the error and provides additional opportunities for practice and review. • If the student repeats the error, the educator identifies the lacking or lagging knowledge, personalizes the presentation of information, and provides more opportunities for practice and review. • **The error is remediated.**	• The educator reminds the student of the rule or expected behavior, states what the student should *not* do, and penalizes the student for exhibiting the undesired behavior. • If the error is repeated, the educator increases the penalty and the interaction becomes a conflict. • **The error is punished.**

9

Creating an Emotionally Safe Learning Climate

Emotional safety means feeling protected, supported, and enabled to take learning risks, make mistakes, and fail without feeling like a failure (Meirovich, 2012; Ryan & Patrick, 2001). When emotional safety is lacking, students fear using their voices in class. You can create a sense of emotional safety by validating students' learning work and helping them to learn from incorrect answers.

The climate of the classroom is as important as the academic content and pedagogical strategies used within it. The emotional climate should be dynamic and result from your awareness of and ability to accurately perceive and manage your own emotions, your students' emotions, and emotional interactions among students and between students and yourself (Mayer & Salovey, 1997; Meirovich, 2012). Developing your mindfulness practice will greatly support your ability to be emotionally present and responsive in the classroom.

Research suggests that the optimal emotional climate of a classroom is predominantly but not always positive, and that matching emotional intensity and arousal to the demands of the learning task is an ongoing matter (Meirovich, 2012). For example, you may want intense positive energy for brainstorming and problem solving, but moderate calm energy for teaching a new lesson with detailed and sequenced steps.

You must constantly be aware of how conducive the emotional climate of the classroom is to learning and be emotionally flexible enough to respond with congruent or complementary emotions. When students are positively engaged and actively contributing, you should respond with the same (congruent) emotions to maintain and reinforce the emotional state that dominates the class. However, when students are hesitant and fearful or bored and fidgety, you should respond with different (complementary) emotions to change the emotional state that dominates the class.

Attending to Equity by Resisting Deficit Beliefs

Many misguided explanations are given for the lower level of academic engagement among Black students as compared to White students (McWhorter, 2000; Ogbu & Fordham, 1986). These deficit hypotheses mistakenly blame students and their families for not valuing and not engaging in school in the same way that middle-class White families do (Valencia, 2012). A more productive strategy is to focus on identifying and understanding ways of increasing student engagement that are under your control (Steele, 2003).

The motivational framework, which states that students' positive and negative emotions about a task and expectations regarding success or failure have a large effect on whether they will engage or avoid learning tasks, provides educators with a psychological lens that is particularly relevant for understanding school disengagement among children coping with trauma (Adelman & Taylor, 2017).

Because Black students are likelier than White peers to be met with punitive and exclusionary discipline (Downey & Pribesh, 2004; Voight et al., 2015), they are also more likely to lose motivation for learning. This can manifest as avoidance, which looks like disruptive and conflictual classroom behaviors. Although social control strategies can temporarily suppress the acting-out behaviors associated with avoidance, without actively reengaging students with classroom learning, unwanted behaviors are likely to reappear. Educators must look below the surface of acting-out behaviors to identify whether avoidance is the cause and provide developmentally supportive responses rather than being unaware of or indifferent to their distress.

Many students fake engagement to avoid punishment. For these students, disengagement shows up as withdrawn, quiet, nonconfrontational behaviors, such as showing polite disinterest in learning activities, shallow discussions with peers during group activities, and religiously following instructions without question or conflict. Too often, educators can lose sight of students exhibiting these disengagement behaviors in classrooms that place a high value on quietness and compliance.

Being disengaged does not mean that a student doesn't value learning. A student who is below grade level in reading may greatly value the idea of improving their reading; they are usually unhappy with their limited skills and know they would feel much better about it if they could read. However, they have also experienced the frustration of trying strategies that have not improved their reading abilities. Thus, they have little to no motivation to try again. They have done it all before, and they still have a reading problem. Sometimes they will do the exercises but just to earn points for a reward or to avoid the consequences of not cooperating. Often, however, they avoid the work, whether by acting out or withdrawing. After all, why should they do things they are certain won't help them read any better? To reengage these students, make sure the learning environment does the following:

1. Minimize threats to feelings of competence, self-determination, and relatedness to valued others. This includes public and competitive assessments of competence.
2. Maximize feelings of competence, self-determination, and connection to others. This includes making school and the classroom feel welcoming, caring, safe, fair, and just.
3. Provide continuous information on learning and performance in ways that highlight growth such that students can receive additional support and direction.

4. Provide opportunities for motivated practice, such as opportunities for meaningful applications of academic content in ways that connect with students' life experiences.

When implemented with consistency, the practices in Figure 9.1 can improve students' perceptions of their educators, the content they are learning, and the work they are expected to produce.

FIGURE 9.1

Practices for Addressing Negative Student Perceptions

If the student thinks . . .	You should . . .
You're not approachable.	Express empathy for any learning challenges and avoid public criticism.
You're not supportive.	Create opportunities to talk with them and understand the motivations for their behaviors.
The content isn't valuable.	Let them help select the content, such as by choosing their own novel with which to practice reading skills.
The content isn't accessible.	Scaffold learning to bridge the gap between their current understandings and grade-level expectations.
An activity or outcome isn't valuable.	Explain how smaller activities have real-life value and build the skills necessary to meet learning goals.
The content isn't accessible or they can't complete an activity.	Scaffold learning to bridge the gap between their current knowledge or skills and the necessary prerequisites to complete the activity.

Encouraging Risk Taking

Remember that it's more important for you to help students get to the correct answer than to evaluate the correctness of their answer. This is especially true of classwide questioning, which is often used to quickly assess learning before moving to the next topic. When assessing the whole class in this way, assure students you will be there to scaffold their learning if they are not yet ready to move on.

Research shows that students benefit from making mistakes and then being supported as they try to correct and learn from them (Kapur & Bielaczyc, 2012; Radatz, 1980). Despite this, U.S. educators tend to ignore errors and praise correct answers (Stevenson & Stigler, 1994; Tulis, 2013). Unfortunately, many educators have been socialized to associate mistakes with shame or embarrassment, viewing them as signs that a student lacks intelligence. Be sure to normalize and show the value of taking learning risks and making the "stretch errors" that are a normal part of learning. When you enthusiastically discuss learning mistakes and reward them as evidence of learning, students are less hesitant and more engaged. Especially in subjects like math that can cause a lot of anxiety, encourage students to make mistakes.

Always keep in mind that students are simultaneously pursuing academic and social goals in the classroom, and most will be hesitant about having their academic contributions judged negatively by their peers. Creating a judgment-free classroom can be done by providing explicit verbal and visual statements about learning being a process that is about much more than getting the correct answer.

Consider an "intentional mistakes" activity to help students see their errors as evidence of learning. Have students work in small groups to answer a challenging question, then provide them with the correct answer and have them identify the different mistakes they made while wrestling with the question. Have each group select one of their mistakes to share and discuss with the whole class.

At the same time, it is important to distinguish between encouraging stretch errors made while trying to learn and discouraging careless errors due to lack of attention. It is also important to ensure that most learning mistakes are not high-stakes mistakes, which are mistakes that are made during exams, especially gatekeeping exams that determine entry into particular programs or schools.

Collaborative Learning

Facilitating student collaboration is about much more than giving students group work activities. During group work and classwide discussions and debates, you must watch for hesitation, fear, disapproval, and ridicule and respond by encouraging acceptance and curiosity and discouraging judgment.

To help students value the academic contributions of others, teach and model the behavior you'd like to see during collaborative learning (Ryan & Patrick, 2001). Students will look to you for signals that they should support rather than compete with their classmates when it comes to academic work. There is much intentionality in the process of creating a collaborative classroom.

Many educators are hesitant to encourage collaboration because they are concerned that it will increase classroom disruptions, but research shows that students do not necessarily become more disruptive when they are encouraged to talk with one another during lessons (Ryan & Patrick, 2001). It is the responsibility of educators to help students work collaboratively, share ideas, and ensure that collaboration is equitable.

One way to do this is by regularly involving the whole class in responding to an individual student's answer. This encourages students to seek one another when they need academic support. When a student answers a question that you have posed to the whole class, invite supportive input from others about whether they agree, have more to add, or can correct a mistake that was made. It is important to validate the student who was brave enough to provide the initial answer. Making this a regular practice in your classroom can strengthen students' perceptions of themselves as being in a community of learners.

To help students understand that classmates are valuable learning resources, encourage them to seek help from one another not only during group work, but also when they are engaged in individual seatwork. Model the use of positive and encouraging language (e.g., "I hear what you are saying, but I do not agree. I think ___.") so that classmates can support one another respectfully.

During successful collaborative learning, all students are engaged, active, sharing their thinking, and validating the thinking of others. They go deep into productive conversations. All students have identified roles and tasks to contribute equally to the project. They get along, have productive conflict, and help one another learn. They know where to find information and know how to get the teacher's attention when they need assistance.

Here are some specific strategies for enabling collaboration among students:

- When possible, place students in groups of four so they can alternate between pair and group work.
- Break large class projects into short-term small-group projects. Rotate team members at the end of each short-term project so that all students get to work with and learn from one another.
- Try to ensure that working groups reflect a cross-section of high and low achievers and students of different genders and ethnicities.
- Regularly pause the whole class to provide instructions for group work when you notice common errors across groups.

Delivering Feedback

Many students see feedback pointing out errors as indicating that they are failures and that the educator dislikes them. The kind of feedback you provide to students will either strengthen or weaken their sense of themselves as learners. Your feedback should show students that you believe in their potential to achieve regardless of their result on any given assignment. Through strategic communication, you can ensure that your corrections strengthen your relationship with students and help them to see a pathway to success in your classroom.

Wise feedback is task-centered rather than person-centered. Provide feedback that affirms the learning process. Do not equate personal worth with doing well academically (e.g., "Good girl, you got all the questions right"), as this primes students to feel low self-worth when they do poorly. The fact is that students coping with trauma are at increased risk of academic failure, and it has nothing to do with whether or not they are good people (Blodgett & Lanigan, 2018; Goodman, Miller, & West-Olatunji, 2012).

Here are some examples of wise feedback:

- "Please review the notes on your practice presentation."
- "Your presentation was well done but can be improved. The expectation for this assignment was that the presentation include _____."
- "Your participation in class has shown me that you know a lot more about this topic than you have included in your presentation."
- "I look forward to your revised presentation incorporating this feedback."

Feedback is most effective when it meets the following criteria:

Genuine. Offer genuine praise often but never so much that it becomes meaningless. Make sure it is sincere. Overly effusive and enthusiastic praise for something simple can alienate students because it is received as insincere.

Constructive. Feedback is constructive when students learn something about what to do differently next time. Saying "That's not correct" or marking an answer with an X can leave students feeling shamed and helpless about how to improve. Feedback should include what was done well, what was incorrect, and suggestions for how they can improve.

Growth-oriented. Acknowledge and praise the learning process, not just the final product. All students should understand that learning new skills improves with practice.

Timely. Students benefit from feedback that is as immediate as possible.

Strategic. Alternate between feedback on what the student has done well with feedback on what needs to be corrected. The goal is maintaining student motivation to work toward improvement.

Equitable. Though some students will necessarily receive more corrective feedback than others, no student should receive only praise or criticism.

Student-led. Before providing your feedback, guide students through the process of reflecting on and providing feedback to a partner or small group, and then provide time for making corrections before submitting assignments. This creates a more enriching learning experience and promotes autonomy.

Multimodal. Feedback can include visual or gestural cues that allow students to correct their mistakes in the moment. These might include a hand signal, pointing to an anchor chart, or silently placing a sticky-note reminder of a correction on the student's work. Gestural cues is especially useful when you are attempting to reduce a repeated error.

Fun. Celebrate effort and progress in ways that are fun or even funny for students. This could include a celebration dance, special handshake, or song. Offer fun or amusing praise after being specific about what students have done well and connecting it to explicit learning expectations.

Caring. Give feedback when you notice something that concerns you about a student, such as a change in their demeanor or general performance (e.g., "I've been noticing ___, and it concerns me because ___"). Sometimes what students need most is knowing that you see them.

Wise feedback should be accompanied by educator self-reflection, especially if you find yourself repeatedly correcting students. Reflect on whether you hold a deficit perspective about the knowledge some students bring to the classroom. You should not attempt to supplant the knowledge and cultural practices that students bring with them into the classroom, but rather build upon them and connect classroom learning to their lives outside school (Milner, 2006). Try to offer every student in your class validation for some aspect of their cultural learning that they bring with them into the classroom. Every student must experience mastery at least once if they are to feel safe taking learning risks. Identify students who have yet to experience success with a lesson or assignment, and create an opportunity for them to demonstrate that their cultural knowledge has value in your classroom.

Helpers Versus Bystanders

Students' sense of emotional safety in your classroom will depend on whether they view you as a helper or a bystander to their school success. As one principal has stated, "Within two weeks of arriving at this school, students can tell which educators like them and which educators do not. They know exactly who will help them and exactly who will make them suffer, without assistance, through the credits necessary to graduate" (Holbrook, 2006). Do you believe that students who fail are at fault for not availing themselves of available supports, or do you believe that your job includes adjusting your supports to match students' needs?

Provide students with second, third, and fourth supported opportunities to experience the feelings of accomplishment associated with successfully completing assignments. There are many skills that students need to learn, and providing multiple opportunities to succeed teaches persistence while also ensuring that they actually learn the academic content. Use questions like these to guide students as they search for correct answers:

- "Explain to me or show me what you've done so far."
- "What resources have you used, so far?"
- "Have you considered ___ or ___?"
- "Think you've tried it all? Let's see. What if we ___?"
- "Watch me do this similar problem."

10

The Possibility of Post-Traumatic Growth

The goal for students experiencing traumatic life experiences should be post-traumatic growth: not merely surviving the trauma but flourishing due to newly developed coping skills. No one should expect to get through this life without having been broken in some way; what matters is how we live with those broken pieces. To thrive despite adversity and trauma is to get through this life as a whole person with many broken pieces welded back together to become stronger than before. The support we receive along the way determines just how successful we ultimately are.

There are three broad domains of post-traumatic growth (Calhoun & Tedeschi, 2014). The first domain involves **developing a more positive perception of oneself and one's abilities.** This usually occurs when individuals come to look upon traumatic events as tests that they were able to survive, affording them greater confidence that they'll be able to withstand future adversities. The second domain is about **more deeply valuing one's relationships with others.** This usually happens when individuals receive enough support to recover their sense of safety and recognize that this support is what enabled them to heal. The third domain has to do with **developing a greater appreciation for life itself.** This occurs when individuals reflect on and reevaluate what really matters in life.

Children and youth are still developing their coping skills and prone to self-blame and shame in the aftermath of interpersonal trauma; therefore, they are especially in need of adult-supported opportunities to process and make meaning. Processing traumatic events is uncomfortable and most attempt to avoid it, but those who are supported to actively lean into the process of meaning making have the chance of gaining a sense of acceptance, agency, and autonomy in the aftermath of trauma. Educators can aid this process by providing learning activities that center narrative construction and reconstruction, such as by reflecting on good and bad life experiences, personal strengths and weaknesses, and dreams for the future (Jayawickreme & Blackie, 2016).

Students coping with trauma don't need you to be their therapist; they need you to respond in ways that align with your role as their educator. This includes (1) making sure students feel seen and heard, (2) making sure they know they can confide in you, (3) helping them make sense of difficult events without blame or shame, and (4) keeping them moving forward by focusing on their strengths.

Making Sure Students Feel Seen and Heard

Making sure students feel seen and heard is one of your primary professional tasks. Children who experience trauma and adversity often feel they're alone because of the shame and silence that come with traumatic experiences, including economic traumas like housing and food insecurity. Children often believe they're the only ones who have experienced what they have. It's also common for children to believe tragic events or family distress is somehow their fault—that they contributed to them with their thoughts, feelings, or actions and that something is wrong with them. These feelings are intensified when the adults in their lives (including their educators) are reluctant to ask about their visible signs of distress.

While acknowledging the challenges that it creates for you and other students in the classroom, remember that acting-out behaviors are often attempts by the student to be seen and heard. Dig deeper to determine whether acting-out behaviors are red flags that something has been missed and questions need to be asked. Keep in mind that some children will attempt to be seen by disappearing from the classroom, in hopes that they will be missed and someone will ask about what may be the cause of their absence.

Making Sure Students Know They Can Confide in You

Many students are left to face their traumas alone despite their visible expressions of distress. Educators don't ask or quickly change the subject because they're afraid they won't have the right words. A "good enough" response first and foremost validates the student's distress and their decision to disclose their trauma. Any student who discloses will be experiencing tremendous fear and uncertainty about whether opening up to you is the right thing to do. They will also be concerned about how they will be judged and what will happen next.

Providing a "good enough" response in the moment is what students in distress need from their educators. As long as your response to students who disclose information about traumatic life events reassures them that (1) it is OK to confide in you, (2) there is no shame or blame in what they are going through, and (3) you will connect them with a staff member who will guide them through what comes next, you are providing a "good enough" response.

Prepare for the moment when a student chooses to disclose a past or ongoing traumatic event by reviewing the following five steps, and determine how to make the suggested statements your own:

1. **Remain calm.** Take comfort in knowing that the student trusts you enough to share this sensitive information. Often, the act of finally sharing is an important part of healing. The student is not necessarily looking for you to solve the problem; they're looking

for you to hear them, accept what they are saying without judgment, and model for them an understanding that problems do have solutions. *Try:* Take gentle, deep breaths throughout the conversation.

2. **Reflectively listen.** Listen attentively and nonjudgmentally to the student. Rephrase what they are saying to ensure that you're understanding them correctly. *Say:* "It sounds like you're saying [a rephrased version of their own words]."

3. **Respond.** Thank the student for bravely sharing what is going on. Give an empathy statement, such as "I'm sorry you are feeling this way" or "I'm sorry that you are having to experience this." Reassure the student that you and others at the school want them to be safe and are here to help. If you will be sharing this information with another staff member or if it falls under mandated reporting guidelines, let the student know that you will be reaching out to others for help. Refrain from making any promises, such as "Everything is going to be alright." If needed, make an appointment to check on the student later that day or week. *Say:* "I'm so sorry you're going through this. It's not your fault."

4. **Reach out.** Contact your school counselor, social worker, or principal in accordance with your school's protocol. If the situation demands immediate attention, such as in the case of suicidal and homicidal ideation, don't leave the student alone. Try to bring in a counselor, social worker, principal, or other support for a direct handoff. *Say:* "I want to help make sure that you're safe, so I need to share this with ___. They know much more about how to help."

5. **Reach back.** Structure reminders for yourself to reach back out to the student and their family as appropriate. If you have made a commitment to calling the student back, do everything in your power to uphold that commitment. *Say:* "I just wanted to check and see how you're doing. It was so brave of you to share."

Many young people who experienced abuse report that they never told, simply because no one ever asked. In many cases, they were hoping for an educator or other adult at school to notice and initiate the discussion. Follow the steps listed above to guide you through these sensitive conversations. Be brave in your willingness to ask students about visible signs of distress, including the quiet signs of neglect.

Helping Students Make Sense of Difficult Events Without Blame or Shame

When your discussions with students help them to make sense of difficult events without any blame or shame, you are engaging in actions that reduce the likelihood of traumatization. Children and youth will find ways to blame themselves for the bad things that happen in their lives. This is developmentally appropriate, because they are in an egocentric stage of development, preoccupied with their own needs and experiences and limited in their awareness of other people's differing realities. Self-blame and shame are common, especially when their family's experiences feel different from others. Children need adults to help them see and believe that there isn't anything wrong with them.

Let the student lead the conversation, listening carefully and correcting misconceptions about self-blame. This may mean that all that happens in the conversation is that the student learns that you recognize they are experiencing some difficulties, that you care, and that you are available to support as best you can.

Keep the following dos and don'ts in mind whenever you are talking with a student who is brave enough to trust you with their story:

- *Do* listen intently and nonjudgmentally and minimize interruptions.
- *Do* believe the student. Take their fears and concerns seriously. It is normal for your initial reaction to be shock or denial, but don't communicate this to the student.
- *Do* reassure the student and emphasize that it's not their fault that something bad has happened. Remind students that they do have adults at school they can talk to.

- *Do* use a strength-based approach in responding. Let them know how courageous they have been in coming forward and highlight their strengths.
- *Do* show compassion while limiting your display of intense emotion, which can overwhelm and can cause them to not express their thoughts or emotions out of concern for upsetting others.
- *Do* be patient and accept uncomfortable silence to allow them to gather thoughts, emotions, and words.
- *Do* let the student know, in words and actions, that all emotions are OK. Let them express their fears and concerns.
- *Do* be clear about the limits to confidentiality. Let them know that you may have to share some of this information with someone who can help more than you can, to try to keep them safe.
- *Don't* try to investigate or provide counseling if this is not your role.
- *Don't* ask a lot of personal details. Once you have a suspicion or confirmation of anything abnormal or unsafe, turn it over to an administrator or counselor to investigate.
- *Don't* tell the student what they could or should have done or ask questions that may lead them to believe they were in any way at fault, such as "Why didn't you tell me?" or "Why were you even there?"
- *Don't* degrade or talk badly about whoever they have identified as a perpetrator. This person may still be someone that they love or care about.
- *Don't* try to connect by saying "I know how you feel." This could distract from what they are sharing, shifting their focus to ways in which you or others couldn't possibly understand the particulars of their experience.
- *Don't* detract from the student's experience by talking about your own experiences at length.
- *Don't* be afraid to admit you don't have an answer. State that you will find out or find someone who can help.
- *Don't* try to fix the problem for the student or tell them what they need to do. It's more empowering to provide them with information and guide them through making their own decisions.

Keeping Students Moving Forward by Focusing on Their Strengths

Helping students find hope and courage for the future by focusing on their strengths is one of the daily acts that you can do in your role as an educator. In the days, weeks, and months after a student discloses, it's important to guard against defining them by their trauma and lowering expectations because of misguided notions of pity. Dr. Shawn Ginwright (2018) calls this "healing-centered engagement," which is a model for how schools can meet the needs of students coping with trauma. He asks educators to view traumatized students as "agents in the creation of their own well-being rather than victims of traumatic events."

You can support healing through your role as an educator by taking a strength-based approach, which balances the understanding that trauma is developmentally damaging with the knowledge that children can be made resilient (McCashen, 2005). Educators must teach the whole child to keep them moving forward academically. A strength-based approach to responding to student disclosures of trauma begins immediately when you acknowledge how courageous students have been in reaching out for help. Point out that the strength and courage they used to talk to you will continue to guide them as they are supported through the trauma.

Educators need to understand just enough about what is happening in students' lives to connect them with the appropriate mental and emotional health support staff, when necessary. Your job is then to provide encouragement and individualized learning adjustments that will enable them to persevere and persist in school as they attempt to manage what is happening outside school.

The simplest way to begin using a strength-based approach is as a reflective practice that encourages you to focus on what students do well, natural talents they display, aspects of the curriculum where they show interest and engagement, and anything else that enables you to think and talk about individual students in terms of their strengths rather than their deficits (Department of Education and Early Childhood Development,

2012). Where you focus your attention will determine both how you see students and how they see themselves (Lopez & Louis, 2009).

A strength-based reflective practice is one where you commit to continuously thinking about whether and how you go about making it impossible for children to fail. This is an equity-focused and action-oriented process of identifying opportunities for students who are experiencing academic or behavioral difficulties to demonstrate mastery. Consider using one of many available low-cost assessments for identifying students' strengths, such as the Clifton Youth Strengths Explorer, the Search Institutes 40 Developmental Assets, or the VIA Inventory of Strengths.

Appendixes

Use the planning sheets and printables in these appendixes to strengthen your use of trauma responsive education practices.

Appendix A
Classroom Vision Statement

Your classroom vision statement should be driven by your philosophy of teaching and learning. It reflects the ways you intend to deliver instruction, manage your classroom, and design your environment and how you want students to feel about themselves, their learning, and their relationships with you and their classmates. This vision should also reflect a classroom that is physically, psychologically, and emotionally safe. Here is one educator's example.

I envision my school and classroom community as a safe haven for all who enter. Students are welcomed, not only by me but also by the warm and supportive environment and by engaging instructional activities that speak to students' unique needs and interests. Students are known, respected, and honored as individuals, with a wealth of experiences, knowledge, and potential.

Students value and support one another in achieving their individual and collective goals. Our behavior management system is based on positive reinforcement, proactive and early intervention, natural consequences, behavioral instruction, and the preserving of relationships. With students as my partners, I will approach behavior management in ways that are both proactive and reflective, identify and address early signs of agitation and emotional and behavioral triggers, and problem-solve together with students and families.

In this classroom, we will learn to recognize, regulate, and support one another in managing strong emotions and thoughts. There are spaces for calming and physical regulation, and alternative seating options to support the needs of high-agitation students. Instructional practices, procedures, and policies will be designed to insist that all students succeed.

Write a vision statement for your trauma responsive classroom:

Appendix B
Vision Statement
Reflection Questions

Reflect on the following questions as you bring your vision into reality.

1. Think of the emotional tone and energy level that you want to feel and exhibit when you walk into your classroom.
   a. Do you feel organized, or do you feel unsure about your plan for the day?
   b. How can you give yourself time to mentally prepare for your day?
   c. What is your morning self-care routine?
   d. How are you using breaks to support and sustain yourself throughout the day?
   e. What about the room makes you feel a sense of belonging?
2. Think of the emotional tone and energy level you want your students to feel and exhibit when they walk into your classroom.
   a. How are you welcoming your students into the room (e.g., standing outside or just inside the door, special class handshake)?
   b. What opening activity gives students an opportunity to discuss their lives (e.g., morning message, greeting at the door, morning meeting)?
   c. What behaviors do you want from students and yourself to make them feel physically, emotionally, and psychologically safe?

3. Think of the feelings that colors convey: yellow is upbeat; red is agitating; blue is calming; green is invigorating. Keep these colors and feelings in mind as you reflect on your vision for your classroom.
   a. Is it most important for your students to be in a classroom with calming, upbeat, or invigorating colors?
   b. How can you create color in your classroom (e.g., bulletin boards, posters, carpet squares)?
4. Think about how you want students to engage with you, with one another, and with the content.
   a. How are your students grouped physically in the classroom?
   b. What are they sitting on and how are they arranged?
   c. How are students sharing information with you and classmates?
   d. What different resources do you have (e.g., manipulatives, technology)?
   e. How do you want students to move within the classroom?
   f. What are the classroom expectations, rules, and consequences?
5. Consider your students' diverse characteristics and backgrounds and reflect on how you will ensure that they see themselves in your classroom. Be intentional about including their culture and ways of being outside school in the classroom.
   a. How does your classroom library celebrate diversity?
   b. What languages are reflected in materials present in your classroom?
   c. How are you building your own cultural competency for yourself and your students?
6. Think about your expectations and whether they are responsive to the needs of students coping with trauma.
   a. How do you handle individual students who struggle with self-regulation?
   b. How do you set up positive classroom expectations and rules?
   c. What are you doing to identify the underlying causes of behavioral challenges?
   d. Are your consequences equitable?
   e. Do you have restorative practices in place?

Appendix C
Your Stress Cues Checklist

Learn your personal stress cues so you can notice when you are being hijacked by stress and find calm. Place a checkmark by cues that may signal that you're becoming distressed.

My Emotional Cues	My Behavior Cues	My Body Cues
I ...	I ...	I ...
☐ Am easily agitated or irritable.	☐ Use harsh words with students and colleagues.	☐ Have nervous energy (e.g., nail biting, fidgeting, pacing).
☐ Am easily frustrated.	☐ Procrastinate.	☐ Have low energy levels.
☐ Have negative and pessimistic thoughts.	☐ Am disorganized and frazzled.	☐ Have difficulty sleeping.
☐ Have difficulty relaxing.	☐ Avoid others.	☐ Have difficulty getting going in the morning.
☐ Am overly critical of myself or others.	☐ Have become increasingly forgetful.	☐ Grind my teeth or clench my jaw.
☐ Don't care about things that are usually important.	☐ Have trouble focusing.	☐ Have headaches.
☐ Feel really sad or down.	☐ Eat too much or too little.	☐ Have unexplained body aches.
☐ Feel an increase in self-doubt.	☐ Have increased alcohol, tobacco, or drug use.	☐ Have tense muscles.
		☐ Feel sick.
		☐ Am getting more colds.

Use the following spaces to create a care plan you can turn to when you notice these cues:

These are the activities that typically help me feel less stressed. Do them!

These are the reminders, affirmations, and encouragement that I most need to hear. Say them!

These are people I can reach out to. Contact them!

For great conversation:

For a good laugh:

To vent:

To cry with me:

For encouragement:

For wisdom and clarity:

Crisis line: 800-273-8255   Text HOME to 741741

Appendix D
Mindfulness Exercise to Reduce Compassion Fatigue

It is important to give yourself the space to release some of the burden that comes from repeatedly engaging with students' dysregulated behaviors—and also recognize opportunities for providing supportive feedback. When you begin to feel compassion fatigue, complete the following reflection to help you leave some of the emotional burden behind at the end of the day.

Part 1

On a day when things feel difficult, take a moment to survey your class. As your eyes rest on each student, take a deep breath and, without judgment, allow yourself to become aware of your feelings toward them. You may have unacknowledged negative feelings about some students.

Part 2

After students have been dismissed for the day and before you leave the building, take 10 minutes to release some of the burden of negative emotions. Take a deep breath as you read each question below, then take several deep breaths as you reflect on your response to each question.

- What are the names of the one, two, or three students about whom you feel the most negative emotions?

- What does each of these students respond positively to; what makes each of them smile?
- What motivates each of these students; when do they get excited and show joy?
- What are each of these students' biggest behavioral struggles?
- What help is each of them asking for through their behaviors?
- What small thing can you do with each of these students tomorrow to show them that they have a place in your classroom?
- Which adults have been able to make even a small connection with each of these students? Can you go to them for help?

Take one final deep breath as you say the following mantra: "I am doing the best I can with the tools I have. My students are doing the best they can with the tools they have. Tomorrow, I will try to learn and teach a new tool."

Appendix E
Weekly Mindfulness Plan

Use the following sample as a model as you create your own weekly mindfulness plan:

Monday	Tuesday	Wednesday	Thursday	Friday
10 mins. morning mindfulness	3–5 mins. morning mindfulness	3–5 mins. morning mindfulness	3–5 mins. morning mindfulness	3–5 mins. morning mindfulness
5 mins. after lunch	3 mins. after PE	5–10 mins. between lunch and library	3 mins. before and 5 mins. after music	5 mins. to end last period

Here is the reasoning for the choices above:

- A longer session on Mondays to regulate after the weekend.
- A session is planned after PE for when students are escalated and need to calm their energy before math class.
- Since students are agitated right after lunch, a session is planned between lunch and library class.
- Students often struggle to calm down during music class, so it begins and ends with a session.

- Students are anxious about stressful events that occur on weekends, so a session is planned for the end of the day.

My Weekly Mindfulness Plan

Monday	Tuesday	Wednesday	Thursday	Friday

My reasoning:

Monday:

_____

Tuesday:

_____

Wednesday:

_____

Thursday:

_____

Friday:

_____

Appendix F
Lunch or Recess Transitions

Many behavior challenges after lunch or recess can be prevented or reduced by intentionally helping students bring their energy and anxiety levels down. Use the following blueprint to transition students back to the classroom. Be sure to model the calm energy level and tone that you want your students to exhibit.

Offer a Warm Greeting

"Good morning/afternoon, students! I am happy to see you (again)! Let's get ready to head back to class."

Settle into Line with a Mindful Moment

Examples for younger students:

First State Expectations

"Let's walk with ears open, eyes forward, voices quiet, hands at your side, and walking feet in your own personal space as we move back to the classroom [or other destination]."

Then Assist Using Words and Modeling

- "Are my scholars ready to move? Let's all do a self-check. Ears open [cups hands behind ears]; eyes forward [points to eyes]; mouths quiet [makes shushing gesture]; hands at my side [holds arms close and stretched down]; and feet in my own space [lifts one leg at a time]."

- "Now, let's take a deep breath in through our noses, filling our lungs slowly to the count of 3: 1 . . . 2 . . . 3. . . . Let it out even more slowly to the count of 6: 1 . . . 2 . . . 3 . . . 4 . . . 5 . . . 6."

Examples for older students:

First State Expectations

"Remember we walk quietly in the halls, keeping hands, feet, objects, and comments to ourselves." It is helpful to designate a student line leader and identify stopping points to reset or reiterate expectations when needed (e.g., stopping before ascending or descending stairs or at the end of the hall before turning corners).

Then Assist Using Words and Modeling

- "Before we walk, let's bring our awareness to the present moment. Look down at your feet, press your toes to the ground, try to feel through your shoes. Next, stretch your fingers out wide in each hand, clench them tight, then relax them at your sides."
- "Now, let's take a deep breath in through our noses, filling our lungs slowly to the count of 3: 1 . . . 2 . . . 3. . . . Let it out even more slowly to the count of 6: 1 . . . 2 . . . 3 . . . 4 . . . 5 . . . 6."

Add "Mindful Moving" Exercises to Your Walk (*optional*)

Mindful Breathing Exercises

- *Rainbow breaths*: Raise arms slowly from the side to above the head and back down.
- *Belly breaths*: Walk with hands on stomach, feeling it contract and expand with each breath.
- Pretend to carry a flower and candle, repeatedly "smelling" it by inhaling deeply and "blowing it out" by exhaling fully.

Focused Attention Exercises

- Have students watch the back of the person in front of them and count the number of deep breaths that person takes. When the transition is finished, have each student show you the count visually (e.g., they can show 2 on one hand and 4 on the other hand for 24). Then give that student a thumbs-up.

- Have students listen for something specific, such as how many educator's voices they hear on the way to their destination. When the transition is finished, ask them to show you how many they heard by raising their fingers.
- Have students look for how many of a particular thing they will pass by the time they reach their destination (e.g., hexagons, things that are blue). When the transition is finished, ask them to show you how many they saw by raising their fingers.

Movement Exercises
- At a predetermined stopping point, stop to face students and have them slowly roll their heads around, once to the left and once to the right, then turn to look to the far right and far left.
- At a predetermined stopping point, lead students in clapping hands together once tightly, rubbing their hands vigorously for a count of 10, and placing their hands on their face to feel the warmth. Students may show with their facial expression how this makes them feel.
- Begin with exaggerated movements (e.g., marching, flapping arms like a chicken), then move gradually to smaller and smaller movements as you get closer to the classroom.

Monitor and Give Feedback

Consider the following types of feedback to give:
- **Verbal praise.** Example: "Nice job moving through the hallway quietly"; "I see you remember our stopping point."
- **Nonverbal praise.** Examples: thumbs-up, head nod, smile, eye wink, shoulder-shimmy celebration
- **Verbal redirections.** Examples:
  - "Let's stop and reset the lines with a slow deep breath in 1, 2, 3 . . . and even slower exhale, 1, 2, 3, 4, 5, 6 . . . and let's begin again."

- "Remember, we move quietly through the halls. (Stop and wait for students to quiet down before moving.) Great, it sounds like we are ready to move."
- *(for younger students)* "Pretend you have a bubble in your mouth and you have to hold that bubble all the way into the classroom."
- **Nonverbal redirections.** Examples:
  - Make eye contact and give a hand signal for any off-task behaviors.
  - Make eye contact and model the correct behavior.
  - Use your proximity to remind students of the expectations and let them know you see and are ready to support them.

Offer a Starter Task and Precorrections

Before your students arrive, be sure to have an immediate starter task ready to engage in learning (e.g., gathering the items needed for the lesson). It is important to also offer precorrections for any regularly occurring behaviors that have not met your expectations.

Examples:
- "As you quietly enter the classroom, go directly to your seat to prepare for our mindful moment before reading. Write down on a sticky note as many words as you can describing your environment: what you hear, smell, see, and so on."
- "As you quietly walk into the room, pick up your journal from your book box and go directly to your own writing space. Reread your last journal entry and make any edits or revisions that you think will improve it." (If all students have to get materials from the same spot, it is best to let them do so a few at a time to reduce congestion that can lead to conflict.)
- "Quietly enter the classroom. Use walking feet to go directly to your desk/table. Silently think about one thing you learned yesterday. Put a quiet thumbs-up on your desk to let me know when you are ready to share."

Appendix G
Self-Regulation Printable

Students need help learning how to name the emotions they feel and how to develop a strategy for reflecting on those emotions before responding. The printable on the next page is an active tool that you can use to help students recognize the physical signs of increasing agitation.

When I notice these signs, I might need to use the calming center

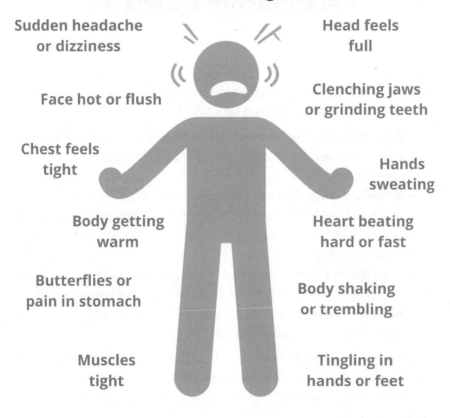

Sudden headache or dizziness

Head feels full

Face hot or flush

Clenching jaws or grinding teeth

Chest feels tight

Hands sweating

Body getting warm

Heart beating hard or fast

Butterflies or pain in stomach

Body shaking or trembling

Muscles tight

Tingling in hands or feet

Appendix H
Relationship Check-In

Complete this classroom relationship check to identify the stage you're in with each student and then act accordingly:

- **Pre-establish stage.** You and the student have had a pattern of conflictual interactions that has laid a foundation of negative emotions and mistrust.
- **Establish stage.** You and the student are neutral in your thoughts about each other or do not yet have a history of interactions that has laid a foundation of trust.
- **Maintain stage:** You are strengthening the good-enough relationships that you have established by intentionally striving for a 5-to-1 ratio of positive praise to behavioral corrections or critique.
- **Restore stage:** You are taking care to continually repair relational harm to established relationships.

Ensure you're being honest with yourself about the status of your relationships by using the table on page 164. At the beginning of each month listed in the table, check off the status of your relationship with each student in your class.

- If you don't have any ideas for breaking the cycle of conflict with students in the pre-establish stage, brainstorm with colleagues.
- Do a classwide "getting to know you" activity to establish relationships with many students at once.

- Maintain good relationships by ensuring that most of your attention doesn't go to students exhibiting acting-out behaviors.
- Act quickly to create opportunities for yourself and students to repair relationships that have been harmed.

Stay motivated by reminding yourself that students coping with trauma may test relationships by lashing out or trying to push you away to see if the relationship can be trusted.

Circle the letter indicating your relationship status with each student:

PR-E = Pre-establish   E = Establish   M = Maintain   R = Restore

Student Name	Relationship Status				
	September	November	January	March	May
1.	Pr-E E M R	Pr-E E M R	Pr-E E M R	Pr-E E M R	Pr-E E M R
2.	Pr-E E M R	Pr-E E M R	Pr-E E M R	Pr-E E M R	Pr-E E M R
3.	Pr-E E M R	Pr-E E M R	Pr-E E M R	Pr-E E M R	Pr-E E M R
4.	Pr-E E M R	Pr-E E M R	Pr-E E M R	Pr-E E M R	Pr-E E M R
5.	Pr-E E M R	Pr-E E M R	Pr-E E M R	Pr-E E M R	Pr-E E M R
6.	Pr-E E M R	Pr-E E M R	Pr-E E M R	Pr-E E M R	Pr-E E M R
7.	Pr-E E M R	Pr-E E M R	Pr-E E M R	Pr-E E M R	Pr-E E M R
8.	Pr-E E M R	Pr-E E M R	Pr-E E M R	Pr-E E M R	Pr-E E M R
9.	Pr-E E M R	Pr-E E M R	Pr-E E M R	Pr-E E M R	Pr-E E M R
10.	Pr-E E M R	Pr-E E M R	Pr-E E M R	Pr-E E M R	Pr-E E M R
11.	Pr-E E M R	Pr-E E M R	Pr-E E M R	Pr-E E M R	Pr-E E M R
12.	Pr-E E M R	Pr-E E M R	Pr-E E M R	Pr-E E M R	Pr-E E M R
13.	Pr-E E M R	Pr-E E M R	Pr-E E M R	Pr-E E M R	Pr-E E M R
14.	Pr-E E M R	Pr-E E M R	Pr-E E M R	Pr-E E M R	Pr-E E M R
15.	Pr-E E M R	Pr-E E M R	Pr-E E M R	Pr-E E M R	Pr-E E M R
16.	Pr-E E M R	Pr-E E M R	Pr-E E M R	Pr-E E M R	Pr-E E M R
17.	Pr-E E M R	Pr-E E M R	Pr-E E M R	Pr-E E M R	Pr-E E M R
18.	Pr-E E M R	Pr-E E M R	Pr-E E M R	Pr-E E M R	Pr-E E M R
19.	Pr-E E M R	Pr-E E M R	Pr-E E M R	Pr-E E M R	Pr-E E M R
20.	Pr-E E M R	Pr-E E M R	Pr-E E M R	Pr-E E M R	Pr-E E M R
21.	Pr-E E M R	Pr-E E M R	Pr-E E M R	Pr-E E M R	Pr-E E M R
22.	Pr-E E M R	Pr-E E M R	Pr-E E M R	Pr-E E M R	Pr-E E M R
23.	Pr-E E M R	Pr-E E M R	Pr-E E M R	Pr-E E M R	Pr-E E M R
24.	Pr-E E M R	Pr-E E M R	Pr-E E M R	Pr-E E M R	Pr-E E M R
25.	Pr-E E M R	Pr-E E M R	Pr-E E M R	Pr-E E M R	Pr-E E M R
26.	Pr-E E M R	Pr-E E M R	Pr-E E M R	Pr-E E M R	Pr-E E M R
27.	Pr-E E M R	Pr-E E M R	Pr-E E M R	Pr-E E M R	Pr-E E M R
28.	Pr-E E M R	Pr-E E M R	Pr-E E M R	Pr-E E M R	Pr-E E M R

Appendix I
Guidelines for Creating Positively Stated Precorrections

Step 1. Think about your class, from student entry to exit. Identify recurring challenges you would like to improve. Describe the situation (time, context, routine, and undesired behaviors).

Time & Location: _____

Context/Routine: _____

_____

Student Behavior: _____

_____

_____

Other factors and information: _____

_____

_____

Step 2. Describe what you want to see instead as replacement behaviors:

_____

_____

_____

_____

Step 3. Identify any modifications to the environment you might make to set students up for success and reduce undesired behavior: _____

_____

_____

_____

_____

Step 4. Identify when and how you will teach replacement behaviors and new routines:

_____

_____

_____

_____

Step 5. Identify specific prompts you will use to precorrect for the expected behavior:

Verbal #1: _____

_____

_____

Verbal #2: _____

_____

_____

Visual/Gestural: _____

_____

_____

What will signal to you that it's time to use the precorrections?

_____

_____

_____

_____

Step 6. Identify how you will praise and provide additional positive reinforcement when students engage in desired behaviors: _____

_____

_____

_____

_____

_____

Step 7. Identify metrics you can use to determine if your plan is working and behaviors are improving: _____

_____

_____

_____

_____

_____

Appendix J
Classroom Experiences Survey

A short and anonymous online survey can help you understand how students are experiencing you and your classroom. This is invaluable information that can help you adjust your environment and your practices to meet students' needs. Build trust with students by discussing what you learn from the survey and how you will make adjustments.

Make an even shorter survey than the one provided using developmentally appropriate language for the lower grades.

Survey

Please complete this anonymous survey so I can learn more about how you are experiencing the class. It will help me ensure that all of us can be successful in this classroom.

Please circle the statement on the right that best reflects how you feel about each item.

In this classroom I feel like . . .			
My teacher really cares about me as a person.	Disagree	Somewhat Agree	Agree
It is safe to ask my teacher for help when I don't understand something.	Disagree	Somewhat Agree	Agree
My teacher understands how I learn best and what I need to be successful.	Disagree	Somewhat Agree	Agree
I feel that my teacher . . .			
Takes the time to listen to my thoughts and feelings.	Disagree	Somewhat Agree	Agree
Expects me to do well in class.	Disagree	Somewhat Agree	Agree
Takes the time to listen to my ideas and suggestions about what we should learn.	Disagree	Somewhat Agree	Agree
In this classroom . . .			
Making mistakes is considered a part of learning.	Disagree	Somewhat Agree	Agree
My teacher encourages me to try again when I get something wrong.	Disagree	Somewhat Agree	Agree
My teacher regularly checks to make sure we understand what they are teaching.	Disagree	Somewhat Agree	Agree
Students in this classroom . . .			
Care about one another.	Disagree	Somewhat Agree	Agree
Treat one another with respect.	Disagree	Somewhat Agree	Agree
Help one another with classroom assignments.	Disagree	Somewhat Agree	Agree

I feel like my teacher . . .			
Helps when I don't understand the homework.	Disagree	Somewhat Agree	Agree
Notices when I am struggling with homework and talks with me about it.	Disagree	Somewhat Agree	Agree

References

Abel, M. H., & Sewell, J. (1999). Stress and burnout in rural and urban secondary school teachers. *Journal of Educational Research, 92*(5), 287–293.

Adelman, H., & Taylor, L. (2017). Addressing barriers to learning: In the classroom and schoolwide. *UCLA's Center for Mental Health in Schools.* http://smhp.psych .ucla.edu/pdfdocs/barriersbook.pdf

Albrecht, N. J., Albrecht, P. M., & Cohen, M. (2012). Mindfully teaching in the classroom: A literature review. *Australian Journal of Teacher Education, 37*(12), n12.

Allday, R. A., & Pakurar, K. (2007). Effects of teacher greetings on student on-task behavior. *Journal of Applied Behavior Analysis, 40*(2), 317–320.

Aloe, A. M., Amo, L. C., & Shanahan, M. E. (2014). Classroom management self-efficacy and burnout: A multivariate meta-analysis. *Educational Psychology Review, 26*(1), 101–126.

Antrop-González, R., & De Jesús, A. (2006). Toward a theory of critical care in urban small school reform: Examining structures and pedagogies of caring in two Latino community-based schools. *International Journal of Qualitative Studies in Education, 19*(4), 409–433.

Baumeister, R. F., Bratslavsky, E., Finkenauer, C., & Vohs, K. D. (2001). Bad is stronger than good. *Review of General Psychology, 5*(4), 323–370.

Beltman, S., Mansfield, C., & Price, A. (2011). Thriving not just surviving: A review of research on educator resilience. *Educational Research Review, 6*(3), 185–207.

Bernard, S. (2010, December 1). To enable learning, put (emotional) safety first. *Edutopia.* www.edutopia.org/neuroscience-brain-based-learning-emotional -safety

Biag, M. (2014). Perceived school safety: Visual narratives from the middle grades. *Journal of School Violence, 13*(2), 165–187.

Blair, C., & Diamond, A. (2008). Biological processes in prevention and intervention: The promotion of self-regulation as a means of preventing school failure. *Development and Psychopathology, 20*(3), 899–911.

Blodgett, C., & Lanigan, J. D. (2018). The association between adverse childhood experience (ACE) and school success in elementary school children. *School Psychology Quarterly, 33*(1), 137–146.

Bloom, S. (1995). Creating sanctuary in the school. *Journal for a Just and Caring Education, 1*(4), 403–433.

Bondy, E., Ross, D. D., Gallingane, C., & Hambacher, E. (2007). Culturally responsive classroom management and more: Creating environments of success and resilience. *Urban Education, 42*, 326–348.

Bordovskaia, N. V., & Baeva, I. A. (2015). The psychological safety of the educational environment and the psychological well-being of Russian secondary school pupils and teachers. *Psychology in Russia, 8*(1), 86.

Borman, G. D., & Dowling, N. M. (2008). Teacher attrition and retention: A meta-analytic and narrative review of the research. *Review of Educational Research, 78*, 367–409.

Broderick, P. C., & Metz, S. M. (2016). Working on the inside: Mindfulness for adolescents. In K. A. Schonert-Reichl & Robert W. Roeser (Eds.), *Handbook of mindfulness in education* (pp. 355–382). Springer.

Brouwers, A., & Tomic, W. (2000). A longitudinal study of teacher burnout and perceived self-efficacy in classroom management. *Teaching and Teacher Education, 16*(2), 239–253.

Brown, K. W., Weinstein, N., & Creswell, J. D. (2012). Trait mindfulness modulates neuroendocrine and affective responses to social evaluative threat. *Psychoneuroendocrinology, 37*(12), 2037–2041.

Butler, L. D., Carello, J., & Maguin, E. (2017). Trauma, stress, and self-care in clinical training: Predictors of burnout, decline in health status, secondary traumatic stress symptoms, and compassion satisfaction. *Psychological Trauma: Theory, Research, Practice, and Policy, 9*(4), 416–424.

Calhoun, L. G., & Tedeschi, R. G. (Eds.). (2014). *Handbook of posttraumatic growth: Research and practice.* Routledge.

Cantor, C. (2009). Post-traumatic stress disorder: Evolutionary perspectives. *Australian & New Zealand Journal of Psychiatry, 43*(11), 1038–1048.

Carlson, E. B., & Dalenberg, C. J. (2000). A conceptual framework for the impact of traumatic experiences. *Trauma, Violence, & Abuse, 1*(1), 4–28.

Carr, S. (January 5, 2022). Why so many Black teachers are leaving the classroom. *Time.* www.time.com/6130991/black-teachers-resigning

Cavanaugh, B. (2016). Trauma-informed classrooms and schools. *Trauma-Informed Classrooms and Schools, 25*(2), 41–46.

Cederblad, M., Dahlin, L., Hagnell, O., & Hansson, K. (1994). Salutogenic childhood factors reported by middle-aged individuals. *European Archives of Psychiatry and Clinical Neuroscience, 244*(1), 1–11.

Chafouleas, S. M., Johnson, A. H., Overstreet, S., & Santos, N. M. (2016). Toward a blueprint for trauma-informed service delivery in schools. *School Mental Health, 8*(1), 144–162.

Chan Tack, A. M., & Small, M. L. (2017). Making friends in violent neighborhoods: Strategies among elementary school children. *Sociological Science, 4*, 224–248.

Chang, M. L. (2009). An appraisal perspective of teacher burnout: Examining the emotional work of teachers. *Educational Psychology Review, 21*(3), 193–218.

Chang, M. L., & Davis, H. A. (2009). Understanding the role of teacher appraisals in shaping the dynamics of their relationships with students: Deconstructing teachers' judgments of disruptive behavior/students. In P. A. Schutz & M. Zembylas (Eds.), *Advances in teacher emotion research* (pp. 95–127). Springer.

Coetzee, S. K., & Klopper, H. C. (2010). Compassion fatigue within nursing practice: A concept analysis. *Nursing & Health Sciences, 12*(2), 235–243.

Collins, K. S. (2001). Children's perceptions of safety and exposure to violence. *International Journal of Adolescence and Youth, 10*(1–2), 31–49.

Compas, B. E. (2006). Psychobiological processes of stress and coping. *Annals of the New York Academy of Sciences, 1094*(1), 226–234.

Cook, A., Spinazzola, J., Ford, J., Lanktree, C., Blaustein, M., Cloitre, M, DeRosa, R., Hubbard, R., Kagan, R., Liautaud, J., Mallah, K., Olafson, E., & van der Kolk, B. (2005). Complex trauma in children and adolescents. *Psychiatric Annals, 35*, 390–398.

Cook, C. R., Coco, S., Zhang, Y., Fiat, A. E., Duong, M. T., Renshaw, T. L., Long, A. C., & Frank, S. (2018). Cultivating positive teacher-student relationships: Preliminary evaluation of the Establish-Maintain-Restore (EMR) method. *School Psychology Review, 47*(3), 226–243.

Cooley-Strickland, M., Quille, T. J., Griffin, R. S., Stuart, E. A., Bradshaw, C. P., & Furr-Holden, D. (2009). Community violence and youth: Affect, behavior, substance use, and academics. *Clinical Child and Family Psychology Review, 12*(2), 127–156.

Cooper, C., & Travers, C. (2012). *Teachers under pressure: Stress in the teaching profession.* Routledge.

Cooper, J. L. (2007). *Facts about trauma for policymakers: Children's mental health.* National Center for Children in Poverty.

Copeland, W., Shanahan, L., Jane Costello, E., & Angold, A. (2009). Configurations of common childhood psychosocial risk factors. *Journal of Child Psychology and Psychiatry, 50*(4), 451–459.

Davidson, R. J., et al. (2003). Alterations in brain and immune function produced by mindfulness meditation. *Psychosomatic Medicine, 65*(4), 564–570.

Department of Education and Early Childhood Development, State of Victoria. (2012). *Strength-based approach: A guide to writing transition learning and development statements.* www.education.vic.gov.au/documents/childhood/professionals/learning/strengthbappr.pdf

Dicke, T., Parker, P. D., Marsh, H. W., Kunter, M., Schmeck, A., & Leutner, D. (2014). Self-efficacy in classroom management, classroom disturbances, and emotional exhaustion: A moderated mediation analysis of teacher candidates. *Journal of Education Psychology, 106*(2), 569–583.

Dods, J. (2013). Enhancing understanding of the nature of supportive school-based relationships for youth who have experienced trauma. *Canadian Journal of Education, 36*(1), 71–95.

Downey, D. B., & Pribesh, S. (2004). When race matters: Teachers' evaluations of students' classroom behavior. *Sociology of Education, 77*(4), 267–282.

Echterling, L. G., Presbury, J. H., & McKee, J. E. (2005). *Crisis intervention: Promoting resilience and resolution in troubled times*. Pearson/Merrill Prentice Hall.

Eidens, A. (2022). 52 parenting affirmations to help you feel positive and empowered each week. *Big Life Journal*. https://biglifejournal.com/blogs/blog/positive-parenting-affirmations

Eldor, L., & Shoshani, A. (2016). Caring relationships in school staff: Exploring the link between compassion and teacher work engagement. *Teaching and Teacher Education, 59*, 126–136.

Evers, W. J., Tomic, W., & Brouwers, A. (2004). Burnout among teachers: Students' and teachers' perceptions compared. *School Psychology International, 25*(2), 131–148.

Fabelo, T., Thompson, M. D., Plotkin, M., Carmichael, D., Marchbanks, M. P., & Booth, E. A. (2011). *Breaking schools' rules: A statewide study of how school discipline relates to students' success and juvenile justice involvement*. Council of State Governments Justice Center.

Figley, C. R. (1995). Compassion fatigue: Toward a new understanding of the costs of caring. In B. H. Stamm (Ed.), *Secondary traumatic stress: Self-care issues for clinicians, researchers, and educators* (pp. 3–28). Sidran Press.

Galla, B. M., Kaiser-Greenland, S., & Black, D. S. (2016). Mindfulness training to promote self-regulation in youth: Effects of the Inner Kids program. In K. A. Schonert-Reichl & Robert W. Roeser (Eds.), *Handbook of mindfulness in education* (pp. 295–312). Springer.

Garmezy, N. (1993). Children in poverty: Resilience despite risk. *Psychiatry, 56*(1), 127–136.

Gaylord-Harden, N. K., Cunningham, J. A., & Zelencik, B. (2011). Effects of exposure to community violence on internalizing symptoms: Does desensitization to violence occur in African American youth? *Journal of Abnormal Child Psychology, 39*(5), 711–719.

Ginwright, S. (2018). The future of healing: Shifting from trauma informed care to healing centered engagement. *Medium*. https://ginwright.medium.com/the-future-of-healing-shifting-from-trauma-informed-care-to-healing-centered-engagement-634f557ce69c

Goodenow, C., & Grady, K. E. (1993). The relationship of school belonging and friends' values to academic motivation among urban adolescent students. *Journal of Experimental Education, 62*(1), 60–71.

Goodman, R. D., Miller, M. D., & West-Olatunji, C. A. (2012). Traumatic stress, socioeconomic status, and academic achievement among primary school students. *Psychological Trauma: Theory, Research, Practice, and Policy, 4*(3), 252.

Grevstad, J. (2007). *Adverse childhood experiences in juvenile justice—Pierce County, WA*. Paper presented at the Family Policy Council Partners Summit, Seattle, Washington.

Gross, J. J. (1998). The emerging field of emotion regulation: An integrative review. *Review of General Psychology, 2*(3), 271–299.

Groves, B., Zuckerman, B., Marans, S., & Cohen, D. (1993). Silent victims: Children who witness violence. *Journal of the American Medical Association, 269*, 262–264.

Hambacher, E. (2018). Resisting punitive school discipline: Perspectives and practices of exemplary urban elementary teachers. *International Journal of Qualitative Studies in Education, 31*(2), 102–118.

Hargreaves, A. (2000). Mixed emotions: Teachers' perceptions of their interactions with students. *Teaching and Teacher Education, 16*(8), 811–826.

Harrell, S. P. (2018). Soulfulness as an orientation to contemplative practice: Culture, liberation, and mindful awareness. *Journal of Contemplative Inquiry, 5*(1), 9–40.

Holbrook C. (2006). Low expectations are the worst form of racism. In J. Landsman & C. W. Lewis (Eds.), *White teachers/diverse classrooms: A guide to building inclusive schools, promoting high expectations, and eliminating racism* (pp. 243–254). Stylus.

Hölzel, B. K., Carmody, J., Vangel, M., Congleton, C., Yerramsetti, S. M., Gard, T., & Lazar, S. W. (2011). Mindfulness practice leads to increases in regional brain gray matter density. *Psychiatry Research: Neuroimaging, 191*(1), 36–43.

Hölzel, B. K., Lazar, S. W., Gard, T., Schuman-Olivier, Z., Vago, D. R., & Ott, U. (2011). How does mindfulness meditation work? Proposing mechanisms of action from a conceptual and neural perspective. *Perspectives on Psychological Science, 6*(6), 537–559.

Homer, E. M., & Fisher, B. W. (2020). Police in schools and student arrest rates across the United States: Examining differences by race, ethnicity, and gender. *Journal of School Violence, 19*(2), 192–204.

Honea, J. M., Jr. (1982). Wait-time as an instructional variable: An influence on teacher and student. *The Clearing House, 56*, 167–170.

Hydon, S., Wong, M., Langley, A. K., Stein, B. D., & Kataoka, S. H. (2015). Preventing secondary traumatic stress in educators. *Child and Adolescent Psychiatric Clinics of North America, 24*(2), 319–333.

Jayawickreme, E., & Blackie, L. E. (2016). *Exploring the psychological benefits of hardship: A critical reassessment of posttraumatic growth.* Springer.

Jennings, P. A. (2015). *Mindfulness for teachers: Simple skills for peace and productivity in the classroom.* W. W. Norton.

Jennings, P. A., & Greenberg, M. T. (2009). The prosocial classroom: Teacher social and emotional competence in relation to student and classroom outcomes. *Review of Educational Research, 79*(1), 491–525.

Jha, A. P., Stanley, E. A., Kiyonaga, A., Wong, L., & Gelfand, L. (2010). Examining the protective effects of mindfulness training on working memory capacity and affective experience. *Emotion, 10*(1), 54.

Kahneman, D., & Riis, J. (2005). Living, and thinking about it: Two perspectives on life. In F. A. Huppert, N. Baylis, & B. Keverne (Eds.), *The science of well-being* (pp. 285–304). Oxford University Press.

Kapur, M., & Bielaczyc, K. (2012). Designing for productive failure. *Journal of the Learning Sciences, 21*(1), 45–83.

Keels, M. (2022). Developmental & ecological perspective on the intergenerational transmission of trauma & violence. *Daedalus, 151*(1), 67–83.

Klassen, R. M. (2010). Teacher stress: The mediating role of collective efficacy beliefs. *Journal of Educational Research, 103*(5), 342–350.

Kleinfeld, J. (1975). Effective teachers of Eskimo and Indian students. *School Review*, *83*, 301–344.

Klem, A. M., & Connell, J. P. (2004). Relationships matter: Linking teacher support to student engagement and achievement. *Journal of School Health, 74*(7), 262–273.

Klusmann, U., Kunter, M., Trautwein, U., Ludtke, O., & Baumert, J. (2008). Teachers' occupational wellbeing and quality of instruction: The important role of self-regulatory patterns. *Journal of Educational Psychology, 100*(3), 702–715.

Koenig, A., Rodger, S., & Specht, J. (2019). Educator burnout and compassion fatigue: A pilot study. *Canadian Journal of School Psychology, 33*(4), 259–278.

Kokkinos, C. M. (2007). Job stressors, personality and burnout in primary school teachers. *British Journal of Educational Psychology, 77*(1), 229–243.

Kopec, D., & Harte, J. D. (2020). Design as the missing variable in trauma-informed schools. In E. Rossen (Ed.), *Supporting and educating traumatized students: A guide for school-based professionals* (pp. 343–357). Oxford University Press.

Kozol, J. (2012). *Savage inequalities. Children in America's schools*. Crown.

Lacoe, J. (2020). Too scared to learn? The academic consequences of feeling unsafe in the classroom. *Urban Education, 55*(10), 1385–1418.

Leek-Openshaw, L. (2011). School-based support group for traumatized students. *School Psychology International, 32*(2), 163–178.

Liew, J., Chen, Q., & Hughes, J. N. (2010). Child effortful control, teacher–student relationships, and achievement in academically at-risk children: Additive and interactive effects. *Early Childhood Research Quarterly, 25*(1), 51–64.

Lomas, T., Medina, J. C., Ivtzan, I., Rupprecht, S., & Eiroa-Orosa, F. J. (2017). The impact of mindfulness on the wellbeing and performance of educators: A systematic review of the empirical literature. *Teaching and Teacher Education, 61*, 132–141.

Lopez, S. J., & Louis, M. C. (2009). The principles of strengths-based education. *Journal of College and Character, 10*(4), 1–8.

Lyins, K. E., & DeLange, J. (2016). Mindfulness matters in the classroom: The effects of mindfulness training on brain development and behavior in children and adolescents. In K. A. Schonert-Reichl & Robert W. Roeser (Eds.), *Handbook of mindfulness in education* (pp. 271–284). Springer.

Ma, X. (2003). Sense of belonging to school: Can schools make a difference? *Journal of Educational Research, 96*(6), 340–349.

Madigan, K., Cross, R. W., Smolkowski, K., & Strycker, L. A. (2016). Association between schoolwide positive behavioural interventions and supports and academic achievement: A 9-year evaluation. *Educational Research and Evaluation, 22*(7–8), 402–421.

Maring, E. F., & Koblinsky, S. A. (2013). Teachers' challenges, strategies, and support needs in schools affected by community violence: A qualitative study. *Journal of School Health, 83*(6), 379–388.

Marzano, R. J., Marzano, J. S., & Pickering, D. (2003). *Classroom management that works: Research-based strategies for every teacher*. ASCD.

Maslow, A. H. (1943). A theory of human motivation. *Psychological Review, 50*, 370–396.

Mayer, J., & Salovey, P. (1997). What is emotional intelligence? In P. Salovey & D. Sluyter (Eds.), *Emotional development and emotional intelligence: Educational implication* (pp. 3–31), Basic Books.

McCashen, W. (2005). *The strengths approach: A strength-based resource for sharing power and creating change.* St. Luke's Innovative Resources.

McCombs, B. (2010). *Developing responsible and autonomous learners: A key to motivating students.* American Psychological Association. www.apa.org/education-career/k12/learners

McLeod, S. (2007). Maslow's hierarchy of needs. *Simply Psychology, 1,* 1–18.

McWhorter, J. (2000). *Losing the race: Self-sabotage in black America.* Free Press.

Meirovich, G. (2012). Creating a favorable emotional climate in the classroom. *International Journal of Management Education, 10*(3), 169–177.

Mendelson, T., Greenberg, M. T., Dariotis, J. K., Gould, L. F., Rhoades, B. L., & Leaf, P. J. (2010). Feasibility and preliminary outcomes of a school-based mindfulness intervention for urban youth. *Journal of Abnormal Child Psychology, 38*(7), 985–994.

Merrill, S. (2017). High school flexible seating done right. *Edutopia.* www.edutopia.org/articles/high-school-flexible-seating-done-right

Mihalas, S., Morse, W. C., Allsopp, D. H., & Alvarez McHatton, P. (2009). Cultivating caring relationships between teachers and secondary students with emotional and behavioral disorders: Implications for research and practice. *Remedial and Special Education, 30*(2), 108–125.

Milner, H. R. (2006). But good intentions are not enough: Theoretical and philosophical relevance in teaching students of color. In J. Landsman & C. W. Lewis (Eds.), *White teachers/diverse classrooms: A guide to building inclusive schools, promoting high expectations, and eliminating racism.* Stylus.

Modinos, G., Ormel, J., & Aleman, A. (2010). Individual differences in dispositional mindfulness and brain activity involved in reappraisal of emotion. *Social Cognitive and Affective Neuroscience, 5*(4), 369–377.

Morelli, L. (2015). *The lemonade hurricane: A story of mindfulness and meditation.* Tilbury House.

National Academies of Sciences, Engineering, and Medicine. (2017). *Community violence as a population health issue: Proceedings of a workshop.* National Academies Press.

National Child Traumatic Stress Network. (2008). *Child trauma toolkit for educators.* Author.

National Scientific Council on the Developing Child. (2010). *Persistent fear and anxiety can affect young children's learning and development* (Working Paper No. 9). Center on the Developing Child.

National Scientific Council on the Developing Child. (2015). *Supportive relationships and active skill-building strengthen the foundations of resilience.* Center on the Developing Child.

Nicole, C. (2016). Black lives matter meditations. [blog post] www.drcandicenicole.com/post/2016-07-black-lives-matter-meditation

Ogbu, J., & Fordham, S. (1986). Black students' school success: Coping with the burden of acting white. *Urban Review, 18*(3), 176–206.

Okonofua, J. A., & Eberhardt, J. L. (2015). Two strikes: Race and the disciplining of young students. *Psychological Science, 26*(5), 617–624.

Okonofua, J. A., Walton, G. M., & Eberhardt, J. L. (2016). A vicious cycle: A social-psychological account of extreme racial disparities in school discipline. *Perspectives on Psychological Science, 11*(3), 381–398.

O'Malley, M. D., & Amarillas, A. (2011). *Perceptions of safety* (What Works Brief #3). WestEd. https://data.calschls.org/resources/S3_WhatWorksBrief3_Safety _final.pdf

Opialla, S., et al. (2015). Neural circuits of emotion regulation: A comparison of mindfulness-based and cognitive reappraisal strategies. *European Archives of Psychiatry and Clinical Neuroscience, 265*(1), 45–55.

Perry, B. D. (2001). The neurodevelopmental impact of violence in childhood. *Textbook of child and adolescent forensic psychiatry,* 221–238.

Perry, B. D. (2006). Fear and learning: Trauma-related factors in the adult education process. *New Directions for Adult and Continuing Education, 110,* 21.

Perry, B. D., Pollard, R. A., Blakley, T. L., Baker, W. L., & Vigilante, D. (1995). Childhood trauma, the neurobiology of adaptation, and "use-dependent" development of the brain: How "states" become "traits." *Infant Mental Health Journal, 16*(4), 271–291.

Price, V. (2006). I don't understand why my African-American students are not achieving. In J. Landsman & C. W. Lewis (Eds.), *White teachers/diverse classrooms: A guide to building inclusive schools, promoting high expectations, and eliminating racism.* Stylus.

Princing, M. (2018). This is why deep breathing makes you feel so chill. *Right as Rain.* https://rightasrain.uwmedicine.org/mind/stress/why-deep-breathing-makes -you-feel-so-chill

Radatz, H. (1980). Students' errors in the mathematical learning process: A survey. *For the Learning of Mathematics, 1*(1), 16–20.

Rak, C. F., & Patterson, L. E. (1996). Promoting resilience in at-risk children. *Journal of Counseling and Development, 74,* 368–373.

Rakic, P. (2009). Evolution of the neocortex: A perspective from developmental biology. *Nature Reviews Neuroscience, 10*(10), 724–735.

Rasmussen, A., Aber, M. S., & Bhana, A. (2004). Adolescent coping and neighborhood violence: Perceptions, exposure, and urban youths' efforts to deal with danger. *American Journal of Community Psychology, 33*(1–2), 61–75.

Regan, K. S. (2003). Using dialogue journals in the classroom: Forming relationships with students with emotional disturbance. *Teaching Exceptional Children, 36,* 36–41.

Ridgard, T. J., Laracu, S. D., Dupaul, G. J., Shapiro, E. S., & Power, T. J. (2015). Trauma-informed care in schools: A social justice imperative. *Communique, 44*(2), 1–15.

Rinke, C. (2007). Understanding teachers' careers: Linking professional life to professional path. *Educational Research Review, 3,* 1–13.

Roeser, R. W., & Peck, S. C. (2009). An education in awareness: Self, motivation, and self-regulated learning in contemplative perspective. *Educational Psychologist, 44*(2), 119–136.

Roorda, D. L., Koomen, H. M., Spilt, J. L., & Oort, F. J. (2011). The influence of affective teacher–student relationships on students' school engagement and achievement: A meta-analytic approach. *Review of Educational Research, 81*(4), 493–529.

Rosanbalm, K. D., & Murray, D. W. (2017). *Caregiver co-regulation across development: A practice brief* (OPRE Brief #2017-80). Office of Planning, Research, and Evaluation, Administration for Children and Families, U.S. Department of Health and Human Services.

Rosen, E., & Hull, R. (2013). *Supporting and educating traumatized students: A guide for school-based professionals.* Oxford University Press.

Ross, D. D., Bondy, E., & Hambacher, E. (2008). Promoting academic engagement through insistence: Being a warm demander. *Childhood Education, 84*(3), 142–146.

Ross, S. W., Romer, N., & Horner, R. H. (2012). Teacher wellbeing and the implementation of school-wide positive behavior interventions and supports. *Journal of Positive Behavior Interventions, 14*(2), 118–128.

Russell, D. W., Altmaier, E., & Van Velzen, D. (1987). Job-related stress, social support, and burnout among classroom teachers. *Journal of Applied Psychology, 72*(2), 269–274.

Ryan, A. M., & Patrick, H. (2001). The classroom social environment and changes in adolescents' motivation and engagement during middle school. *American Educational Research Journal, 38*(2), 437–460.

Ryan, C. O., Browning, W. D., Clancy, J. O., Andrews, S. L., & Kallianpurkar, N. B. (2014). Biophilic design patterns: Emerging nature-based parameters for health and well-being in the built environment. *International Journal of Architectural Research, 8*(2), 62–76.

Ryff, C. D., & Singer, B. (2003). Flourishing under fire: Resilience as a prototype of challenged thriving. *Flourishing: Positive Psychology and the Life Well-Lived*, 15–36.

Schetter, C. D., & Dolbier, C. (2011). Resilience in the context of chronic stress and health in adults. *Social and Personality Psychology Compass, 5*(9), 634–652.

Schore, A. N. (2003). *Affect regulation and the repair of the self.* W. W. Norton.

Schwab-Stone, M. E., Ayers, T. S., Kasprow, W., Voyce, C., Barone, C., Shriver, T., & Weissberg, R. P. (1995). No safe haven: A study of violence exposure in an urban community. *Journal of the American Academy of Child & Adolescent Psychiatry, 34*(10), 1343–1352.

Sharkey, P. (2010). The acute effect of local homicides on children's cognitive performance. *Proceedings of the National Academy of Sciences, 107*(26), 11733–11738.

Sheinman, N., Hadar, L. L., Gafni, D., & Milman, M. (2018). Preliminary investigation of whole-school mindfulness in education programs and children's mindfulness-based coping strategies. *Journal of Child and Family Studies, 27*(10), 3316–3328.

Shonkoff, J. P., et al. (2012). The lifelong effects of early childhood adversity and toxic stress. *Pediatrics, 129*(1), e232–e246.

Siegel, D. J. (2007). Mindfulness training and neural integration: Differentiation of distinct streams of awareness and the cultivation of wellbeing. *Social Cognitive and Affective Neuroscience, 2*(4), 259–263.

Siegel, D. J., Siegel, M. W., & Parker, S. C. (2016). Internal education and the roots of resilience: Relationships and reflection as the new *R*s of education. In K. A. Schonert-Reichl & Robert W. Roeser (Eds.), *Handbook of mindfulness in education* (pp. 47–63). Springer.

Singh, N. N., Lancioni, G., Winton, A., Karazsia, B., & Singh, J. (2013). Mindfulness training for teachers changes the behavior of their preschool students. *Research in Human Development, 10*(3), 211–233.

Skaalvik, E. M., & Skaalvik, S. (2015). Job satisfaction, stress and coping strategies in the teaching profession: What do teachers say? *International Education Studies, 8*(3), 181–192.

Skiba, R. J., Horner, R. H., Chung, C. G., Rausch, M. K., May, S. L., & Tobin, T. (2011). Race is not neutral: A national investigation of African American and Latino disproportionality in school discipline. *School Psychology Review, 40*(1), 85.

Skiba, R. J., Michael, R. S., Nardo, A. C., & Peterson, R. L. (2002). The color of discipline: Sources of racial and gender disproportionality in school punishment. *The Urban Review, 34*(4), 317–342.

Skinner, E., & Beers, J. (2016). Mindfulness and teachers' coping in the classroom: A developmental model of teacher stress, coping, and everyday resilience. In K. A. Schonert-Reichl & Robert W. Roeser (Eds.), *Handbook of mindfulness in education* (pp. 99–118). Springer.

Smith, B. (n.d.). Social-emotional learning and academics. *Committee for Children.* www.cfchildren.org

Smith, V., & Jelen, M. (2016). Mindfulness activities and interventions that support special populations. In K. A. Schonert-Reichl & Robert W. Roeser (Eds.), *Handbook of mindfulness in education* (pp. 171–190). Springer.

Society for Research in Child Development. (2009). *Healthy development: A summit on young children's mental health.* Author.

Solar, E. (2013). An alternative approach to behavior interventions: Mindfulness-based stress reduction. *Beyond Behavior, 22*(2), 44–48.

Souers, K., & Hall, P. (2016). *Fostering resilient learners: Strategies for creating a trauma-sensitive classroom.* ASCD.

Southern Poverty Law Center. (2019) *Let's talk: Discussing race, racism and other difficult topics with students.* www.tolerance.org/sites/default/files/general/TT%20Difficult%20Conversations%20web.pdf

Sparks, D. (2016, August 4). How feeling respected transforms a student's relationship to school. *Education Week.* www.pbs.org/newshour/education/feeling-respected-transforms-student-school

Staats, C. (2014). Implicit racial bias and school discipline disparities. *Kirwan Institute Special Report.* http://kirwaninstitute.osu.edu/wp-content/uploads/2014/05/ki-ib-argument-piece03.pdf

Stanley, D. A., Sokol-Hessner, P., Banaji, M. R., & Phelps, E. A. (2011). Implicit race attitudes predict trustworthiness judgments and economic trust decisions. *Proceedings of the National Academy of Sciences, 108*(19), 7710–7715.

Steele, C. (2003). Race and the schooling of Black Americans. In S. Plous (Ed.), *Understanding prejudice and discrimination* (pp. 98–107). McGraw-Hill.

Stevenson, H., & Stigler, J. W. (1994). *Learning gap: Why our schools are failing and what we can learn from Japanese and Chinese education.* Simon & Schuster.

Storch, E. A., & Crisp, H. L. (2004). Introduction: Taking it to the schools—transporting empirically supported treatments for childhood psychopathology to the school setting. *Clinical Child and Family Psychology Review, 7*(4), 191–193.

Sue, D. W. (Ed.). (2010). *Microaggressions and marginality: Manifestation, dynamics, and impact.* Wiley.

Terada, Y. (2021, March 26). Why Black teachers walk away. *Edutopia.* www.edutopia .org/article/why-black-teachers-walk-away

Tomlinson, C. A., & McTighe, J. (2006). *Integrating differentiated instruction & understanding by design: Connecting content and kids.* ASCD.

Tornio, S. (2018, August 28). 30 ways to bring more mindfulness and self-care to your classroom. *We Are Teachers.* www.weareteachers.com/classroom-self-care

Tulis, M. (2013). Error management behavior in classrooms: Teachers' responses to student mistakes. *Teaching and Teacher Education, 33,* 56–68.

Valencia, R. R. (2012). *The evolution of deficit thinking: Educational thought and practice.* Routledge.

Van der Kolk, B. A. (2015). *The body keeps the score: Brain, mind, and body in the healing of trauma.* Penguin Books.

Voight, A., Hanson, T., O'Malley, M., & Adekanye, L. (2015). The racial school climate gap: Within-school disparities in students' experiences of safety, support, and connectedness. *American Journal of Community Psychology, 56*(3), 252–267.

Wegner, D. M. (1994). Ironic processes of mental control. *Psychological Review, 101*(1), 34.

Welch, K., & Payne, A. A. (2010). Racial threat and punitive school discipline. *Social Problems, 57*(1), 25–48.

Wentzel, K. R. (1997). Student motivation in middle school: The role of perceived pedagogical caring. *Journal of Educational Psychology, 89*(3), 411.

West, S., Day, A., Somers, C., & Baroni, B. (2014). Student perspectives on how trauma experiences manifest in the classroom: Engaging court-involved youth in the development of a trauma-informed teaching curriculum. *Children & Youth Services Review, 38,* 58–65.

Williams, J. M., & Kabat-Zinn, J. (2013). *Mindfulness: Diverse perspectives on its meaning, origins and applications.* Routledge.

Wilms, L., & Oberfeld, D. (2018). Color and emotion: Effects of hue, saturation, and brightness. *Psychological Research, 82*(5), 896–914.

Wilson, B. L., & Corbett, H. D. (2001). *Listening to urban kids: School reform and the teachers they want.* State University of New York Press.

Wolpow, R., Johnson, M. M., Hertel, R., & Kincaid, S. O. (2009). *The heart of learning and teaching: Compassion, resiliency, and academic success.* Office of Superintendent of Public Instruction (OSPI) Compassionate Schools.

Woodward, C., & Joseph, S. (2003). Positive change processes and post-traumatic growth in people who have experienced childhood abuse: Understanding vehicles of change. *Psychology and Psychotherapy: Theory, Research and Practice, 76*(3), 267–283.

Yosso, T. J., Smith, W. A., Ceja, M., & Solórzano, D. G. (2009). Critical race theory, racial microaggressions, and campus racial climate for latina/o undergraduates. *Harvard Educational Review, 79*(4), 659–690.

Zee, M., & Kooman, H. M. Y. (2016). Teacher self-efficacy and its effects on classroom processes, student academic adjustment, and teacher wellbeing: A synthesis of 40 years of research. *Review of Educational Research, 86*(4), 981–1015.

Index

The letter *f* following a page locator denotes a figure.

About the Author

Micere Keels is an associate professor at the University of Chicago and the founding director of the Trauma Responsive Educational Practices Project (TREP Project). For over two decades, she has worked to integrate mental health promotion interventions into educational systems and structures, from early childhood centers to high schools. The TREP Project works to develop the individual and organizational capacity of educators and schools serving children growing up in neighborhoods that have high levels of toxic stress, such as violent crime, concentrated poverty, concentrated foster care involvement, and housing instability. Through the TREP Project, Dr. Keels has supported the professional development of over 200,000 educators through school district partnerships in Delaware, Illinois, New York, Ohio, and Rhode Island, and through work with many individual schools across the United States.

Related ASCD Resources: Trauma-Informed Instruction

At the time of publication, the following resources were available (ASCD stock numbers in parentheses).

Creating a Trauma-Sensitive Classroom (QRG) by Kristin Van Marter Souers and Pete Hall (#QRG118054)

Fostering Resilient Learners: Strategies for Creating a Trauma-Sensitive Classroom by Kristin Van Marter Souers and Pete Hall (#116014)

Hanging In: Strategies for Teaching the Students Who Challenge Us Most by Jeffrey Benson (#114013)

How to Reach the Hard to Teach: Excellent Instruction for Those Who Need It Most by Jana Echevarría, Nancy Frey, and Douglas Fisher (#116010)

Relationship, Responsibility, and Regulation: Trauma-Invested Practices for Fostering Resilient Learners by Kristin Van Marter Souers and Pete Hall (#119027)

Restoring Students' Innate Power: Trauma-Responsive Strategies for Teaching Multilingual Newcomers by Louise El Yaafouri (#122004)

Teaching and Supporting Students Living with Adversity (QRG) by Debbie Zacarian and Lourdes Alvarez-Ortiz (#QRG120035)

Teaching to Strengths: Supporting Students Living with Trauma, Violence, and Chronic Stress by Debbie Zacarian, Lourdes Alvarez-Ortiz, and Judie Haynes (#117035)

Trauma-Invested Practices to Meet Students' Needs (QRG) by Kristin Van Marter Souers and Pete Hall (#QRG119077)

Trauma-Informed Teaching and IEPs: Strategies for Building Student Resilience by Melissa Sadin (#122026)

Trauma-Sensitive School Leadership: Building a Learning Environment to Support Healing and Success by Bill Ziegler, Dave Ramage, Andrea Parson, and Justin Foster (#122013)

For up-to-date information about ASCD resources, go to www.ascd.org. You can search the complete archives of *Educational Leadership* at www.ascd.org/el.

ASCD myTeachSource®

Download resources from a professional learning platform with hundreds of research-based best practices and tools for your classroom at http://myteachsource.ascd.org

For more information, send an email to member@ascd.org; call 1-800-933-2723 or 703-578-9600; send a fax to 703-575-5400; or write to Information Services, ASCD, 2800 Shirlington Rd., Suite 1001, Arlington, VA 22206 USA.

THE WHOLE CHILD

The ASCD Whole Child approach is an effort to transition from a focus on narrowly defined academic achievement to one that promotes the long-term development and success of all children. Through this approach, ASCD supports educators, families, community members, and policymakers as they move from a vision about educating the whole child to sustainable, collaborative actions.

Trauma Responsive Educational Practices relates to the **engaged**, **safe**, and **supported** tenets.

For more about the ASCD Whole Child approach, visit **www.ascd.org/wholechild.**

WHOLE CHILD
TENETS

1 **HEALTHY**
Each student enters school healthy and learns about and practices a healthy lifestyle.

2 **SAFE**
Each student learns in an environment that is physically and emotionally safe for students and adults.

3 **ENGAGED**
Each student is actively engaged in learning and is connected to the school and broader community.

4 **SUPPORTED**
Each student has access to personalized learning and is supported by qualified, caring adults.

5 **CHALLENGED**
Each student is challenged academically and prepared for success in college or further study and for employment and participation in a global environment.

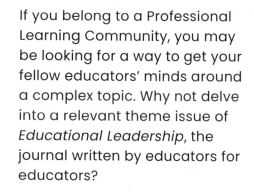